Adlai E. Stevenson and American Intellectuals

C. Baars Bultman

Adlai E. Stevenson and American Intellectuals

The Terms of Endearment

C. Baars Bultman
Interdisciplinary Studies, History, Political Science, Education
Hope College Professor Emeritus
Saugatuck, USA

ISBN 978-3-031-80647-6   ISBN 978-3-031-80648-3   (eBook)
https://doi.org/10.1007/978-3-031-80648-3

This Palgrave Macmillan imprint is published by the registered company Springer Nature Switzerland AG.
The registered company address is: Gewerbestrasse 11, 6330 Cham, Switzerland

If disposing of this product, please recycle the paper.

To Margo—Always Here
and
James Seaton, Extraordinary Mentor, in Memoriam

Acknowledgments

Any reader of this modest work will recognize myriad citations and references to the many historians, who singularly, and collectively, have left a comprehensive body of knowledge about Adlai Stevenson's life and work. I am grateful to all of them for inspiring me to offer yet another interpretation.

This project would not have even begun without the early support of scholars at Michigan State University. In addition to James Seaton, I am professionally indebted to Lisa Fine, Jim McClintock, Robert Martin (in memoriam), and Douglas Hoekstra (in memoriam), all of whom thought this story was worth telling. My sincere thanks also to playwright and librettist Sandra Seaton and my former colleagues at Hope College: Richard and Barbara Mezeske, for their encouragement. For their hospitality and research advice, I also thank Katherine Hamilton-Smith and Nicole Stocker both associated with the Stevenson Center on Democracy and the Lake County Forest Preserves in Illinois.

Projects such as this one would never be successfully concluded without the guidance of the ever-attentive editorial and production teams at Palgrave Macmillan. With sincere gratitude, I thank History Editor Carly Silver, who saw potential in the original manuscript and supplied momentum, Humanities Editor Anita Rachmat, and Production Editors Sujatha Mani, Sheejha Attassery Balasubrahmanian, and their staff. Their expertise and patience were necessary every step of the way. Thanks, too, to Big Blue Water, LLC for their technical assistance.

Saugatuck, Michigan

CONTENTS

Photo of framed print of Norman Rockwell's *Adlai Stevenson* (*Post*, October 6, 1956)

Introduction

Abstract Chapter 1 introduces the unique position that Adlai Stevenson holds in United States' cultural, intellectual, and political history. It also highlights the purposes of the book and its intended readership.

Keywords Cultural • Intellectual • Political • Interdisciplinary

In Garry Trudeau's December 1, 1984, Doonesbury cartoon, Rick Redfern, a principal character, is bedridden by his despair over the recent election results in which Ronald Reagan retained the Presidency. Trudeau concludes a verbal exchange sequence in the final frame with Rick saying to Joanie, "If something happens to me, you must tell our son about Adlai Stevenson!" Perhaps then, nearly two decades after his death, and certainly today, Stevenson is too often a mere footnote in American cultural, intellectual, and political history. Twenty-first century crossword players are likely baffled by "'Five letters down, beginning with "A" and ending in "i'." And one has to be of a certain age to appreciate the slogan "Madly for Adlai." This was not always so. The author's hope is that this book will help readers become acquainted with Adlai E. Stevenson II, and in other cases deepen their knowledge of his unique, somewhat non-political, role in American culture as highlighted in subsequent chapters. The book will be especially attractive to readers interested in the often-underplayed intersection of American history, American literature, and American

C. B. Bultman, *Adlai E. Stevenson and American Intellectuals*,
https://doi.org/10.1007/978-3-031-80648-3_1

1

politics. Essentially, it could be considered an interdisciplinary book for an interdisciplinary readership. Of special note is that 2025 will mark the 125th year of Stevenson's birth (February 5, 1900) and the 60th year since his death (July 14, 1965).

As R.W. Apple, Jr., Chief Washington Correspondent for the *New York Times*, surveyed the political culture of the United States prior to the 2000 President Election, he remarked that "not since 1968 when poet-politician Senator Eugene J. McCarthy flew to Chicago for the doomed Democratic National Convention with the poet Robert Lowell and the novelist William Styron in his private plane, has a high-profile American politician…so publicly associated himself with symbols of Art" (Apple 2). Another twentieth-century American politician mentioned by Apple as having celebrated his association with the intellectual world was Adlai E. Stevenson II, the Presidential nominee of the Democratic Party in 1952 and 1956.

When I was a seventeen-year-old high school history student in 1965, Mr. David Anderson, my teacher, began the year invoking the name of Adlai Stevenson as "the smartest man never to be elected President of the United States." Stevenson had died just six weeks earlier, and the instructor felt compelled to ensure that his students knew of him. Until that moment, I had not thought about Stevenson for years. During the campaign of 1956, I had jostled with another boy in a Muskegon, Michigan, alleyway because he was wearing a "Stevenson for President" button.

Since I came from a staunchly Republican family, and one which believed that Dwight Eisenhower was, at the very least, a demi-god, my action seemed warranted at the time. Ike won his battle while I did not. The way that Mr. Anderson spoke of Stevenson that day left an impression, and, more importantly, it sparked an interest in Stevenson that remains to this day.

"The smartest man never to be elected President." Why would my teacher say such a thing? Are not all presidents assumed to be intelligent? If Stevenson were so "smart," why did not the people elect him? And by what criteria was he deemed intelligent anyway? What kinds of people supported a man like Stevenson, at least perceiving him to be more intelligent than his opponents? Trying to adequately answer such questions has been truly an intellectual journey. For roughly sixty years, I have been reading about Adlai Stevenson; and now, finally, I write, in part, to contribute something new and at the very least, under-examined, in Stevenson scholarship, but also to inform and attract a more general readership to an interesting and unique cultural critique.

To pretend that this work is simply objective clinical research would be less than truthful. My interest in Stevenson as a subject has taken me to his boyhood home on East Washington Street in Bloomington, Illinois, and his gravesite at Evergreen Cemetery across town. I have made the excursion to his farm near Libertyville, Illinois, where I persuaded Lake County Forest Preserve employees to allow me to roam at will through the then unoccupied house. I have stood where Stevenson died near Grosvenor Square in London. I confess that at each location I have been stirred in some way by the mythology that surrounds his character. Still, the purpose of this project is not to elevate, embellish, or idealize Stevenson almost sixty years after his death. The long game of history is, after all, already littered by sometimes hollow and misappropriated encomia.

Adlai Stevenson was a complex figure in American public life. He remains enigmatic today. Both extollers and detractors admit as much in finding him at once liberal and conservative, political machinist, and aloof novice, sensitive to the plight of the dispossessed and social dandy. The seed of this book has been a lingering curiosity about a man and his place in American culture, and my own continuing personal entanglement with a rather perplexing public figure.

To be clear, this study is not specifically a political history dealing with questions of institutional governance. A reader who looks at this book through the pure lens of political science, for example, could be disappointed, as it is not primarily about presidential politics in the 1950s and is not driven by direct considerations of statistical analysis of voter behavior, nor with questions of why Stevenson did so poorly in his two battles with Eisenhower. He lost the electoral vote 442–89 in 1952, and 457–73 in 1956. Similarly, a historian of economics, who seeks insight into Stevenson's role in regional and national policy positions regarding the production and distribution of goods and services, may have limited interest in this book. The analysis herein is predominantly qualitative, rather than quantitative. Perhaps this book will be best classified as both a cultural history and an intellectual history; cultural history because it is referent to ideas, values, and the expressions of human beings in aesthetic works, and as intellectual history because it reveals ideas, beliefs, and theories about topics which were thought to be important in a time and place. That said, this narrative of course, could not disregard political framing.

Adlai Stevenson was, after all, a prominent presence on the American political stage in the 1950s and early 1960s, right up to his death in 1965. This book is not about whether Stevenson would have made a great, or even a good President; nor is it primarily about whether Stevenson was, by acceptable definition, an intellectual; it does, however, highlight the perceptions of intellectuals about Stevenson's capacity on both counts. Furthermore, it was not my primary task to dissect Stevenson's writings and speeches looking for the evolution of his thinking on any number of national and international dilemmas. These areas of inquiry are interesting and have merit as they stand, but development of them was not my goal. Additionally, all of the considerations mentioned in these prior paragraphs have been thoroughly and meticulously addressed previously by many historians, political scientists, and Stevenson's closest friends.

Although this study does not focus on political events or social trends of the 1950s, some historical grounding can be helpful. Eugene McCarthy once said of Adlai Stevenson that he "was not ahead of his times, or outside of his times, as some of his critics said. He was a contemporary" (McCarthy 213). Any discussion of Stevenson, then, will necessarily place him to some degree against the backdrop of the era in which he lived. Stevenson's putative identification as an "intellectual," for example, becomes more significant if one accepts the notion that the decade was essentially anti-intellectual, a period in which historian Eric Goldman wrote that "people were beginning to use the word 'intellectual' as if it meant some compound of evil, stupidity, and treason" (Goldman 123). Or, as a University of Utah professor said after the election of 1952: "The whole era is ended, is totally repudiated, a whole era of brains and literacy and exciting thinking" (235). Former President Harry Truman wrote privately that Stevenson was "damned regularly by Republicans, and I've got to admit with regret, by a lot of Democrats as well—as being that truly terrible thing, an intellectual" (Truman 59). Similarly, historian Arthur M. Schlesinger, Jr.'s judgment of Eisenhower as the symbol and expression of "a national desire for repose" (Schlesinger, "Politics" 220) helps us to understand, in part, why many voters opted for him instead of Stevenson. Schlesinger suggested that "any activist President would have encountered difficulty in the 1950s.... The Fifties were certainly a time when the cycle was in a phase of quiescence," adding that "if Adlai Stevenson had been elected in 1952, he probably would have encountered frustration.... Eisenhower unquestionably suited the national mood" (270). To be sure,

Stevenson's wit and erudition ran counter to an era famous for its blandness.

Twenty years earlier (1950), and Eisenhower not yet in the White House, Schlesinger also provided another useful critique for understanding the decade ahead. He concluded that the liberalism of the New Deal interventionist state had become the "vital center" of American political life, "providing a lighted path between the darkness of left and right philosophies" (Gilbert 235). The liberalism of the "vital center," according to Schlesinger, was the antidote for the political sterility of extremism only if a "new virility" infused it (235). Since many of the basic tenets of the "vital center" were shared by both Democrats and Eisenhower Republicans, classifying Stevenson as a "liberal" is problematic, as I try to show in Chap. 3, especially because his political virility was sometimes questioned.

The decided focus of this study is a biographical rendering of Stevenson's alliance with a segment of the intellectual community, with a primary focus on the years from 1940 to his death in 1965. At the core of the investigation is an evaluation of the nature of a relationship that was important both to intellectuals, particularly literary-intellectuals, whom Irving Howe called, "Mr. Stevenson's little bodyguard of friends and admirers, with their literary contacts and facilities for the projection of their views," (Howe, "Stevenson," 11), and who came to believe that Adlai Stevenson's spoken and written words were the central instruments of his intellect. Separate chapters are devoted to literary-intellectuals at large and to Archibald MacLeish and John Steinbeck, in particular. The book will be most useful and relevant to readers who are curious as to why the relationship was so important and endearing to both.

Chapter 2 necessarily begins with the problem of arriving at a suitable working definition of the term "intellectual." The second chapter also reviews the historic dilemmas which face intellectuals who seek public office and those who may get "too close" to it as well. In reviewing these dilemmas several questions emerge, none of them easy to answer. Why is there less public acceptance of intellectuals in politics in the United States than in many other countries? How can intellectuals use politics without being used by it? How serious are the dangers to intellectuals when they subordinate the problems of craft to matters of public policy? Which is more deleterious for intellectuals, both individually and as a group: to exercise no political voice or to sacrifice artistic ambition? Can we expect intellectuals to be dispassionate? Do they expect themselves to be dispassionate? Do true intellectuals allow themselves to stray from their own fields? All of this helps to provide the framework for the essential question. During Stevenson's Presidential campaigns, including his quixotic run in 1960, many intellectuals, who characteristically disabused political life, pursued pro-active roles in public political circles and were willingly distracted from their craft. Why?

Chapter 3 reviews in some detail Stevenson's own intellectual development, as well as his relationships within the American intellectual community in general. Chapter 4 is devoted entirely to a key reason for Stevenson's endearment to intellectuals: the co-equal manner in which he treated them. That ingredient in their relationship has elsewhere been given scant development. The fifth and sixth chapters serve as a more explicit representation of intellectuals' affinity for Stevenson. These are case studies which illumine the alliance through a close examination of Stevenson's special relations with American writers Archibald MacLeish and John Steinbeck, and feed the conclusions in Chap. 7.

Richard Holmes, England's leading Romantic biographer, said that for him "biography has always been a personal adventure of exploration and pursuit" (Lee 53). So, too, it has been for me. Holmes was correct in believing that biography is never monolithic, never conclusive, or definitive, but always in motion (53). With Stevenson, this is surely the case. He continues to be written about, sometimes in comprehensive studies, but more frequently in short references, nearly always linking Stevenson to a style, to elevated discourse, to the accolades of intellectuals. For now, my claim that this book offers something "fresh" or "unique" or "breaks new ground" in the Stevenson literature seems to hold up. While they may give some attention to Stevenson's relationship with intellectuals in general, none of the existing studies seems to bring it front and center, accentuated by case studies, like this narrative attempts to do. Noteworthy, too, is that Alvin Liebling's *Adlai Stevenson's Lasting Legacy* (2007, Palgrave Macmillan) appears to be the most recent full-length book published about Stevenson.

As the 2000 presidential campaign was gaining momentum, and within days of Stevenson's centenary, historian Richard Norton Smith wrote that candidate Senator Bill Bradley had been "recast as a victim of his own virtues. Too cerebral. Too reluctant to hit back.... In short, too Stevensonian." The same might have been said about Eugene McCarthy, who, incidentally, nominated Stevenson for President at the 1960 Democratic National Convention in Los Angeles, momentarily stirring again the hopes of American intellectuals. In her recently published memoir of the 1960s, historian Doris Kearns Goodwin recalls her husband Richard Goodwin as saying of McCarthy, "'He was more often keen to talk about a new poem with friend and fellow poet, Robert Lowell, than to plot campaign strategy'" (Goodwin, Doris 321). "Though a pejorative today [Stevensonian]," wrote Smith, "back then [1950s] his name conjured up a civility rare in public life.... That his name has become a synonym for honorable futility is a sobering comment on [the] electorate. Often disappointed, Stevenson was never disillusioned. Would that the modern voter could say as much" (Smith 15). Alistair Cooke, the English born American journalist and Stevenson friend, wrote that "Adlai Stevenson remains the liveliest reminder of our time that there are admirable reasons for failing to be president" (Cooke 151).

In the 1990 PBS documentary, *Adlai Stevenson: The Man from Libertyville*, Stevenson's eldest son, Adlai III, lamented that he did not think "someone like my father was possible today" [at the highest level of American political office]. As American citizens prepared themselves for the maelstrom of the 2024 presidential campaign, Adlai III's worry seems credible. The behaviors some of the candidates and those who support them represents an accelerating cultural shift away from civility, decency, dignity, and grace in public life. Politics has never been entirely free from a certain coarseness, but the current depth of it, and, significantly, the level of tolerance toward it, is troubling. As will be evident from the narrative that follows, Adlai Stevenson II was a political being from a long family, political lineage (his grandfather Adlai Stevenson I was Vice-President under Grover Cleveland) and quite capable of all the give and take in a rough-and-tumble political world and should be judged accordingly. In the same documentary, *New York Times* writer, James Reston said of Stevenson that he was sometimes ridiculed for his formality, his sophisticated way of speaking, his genteel nature, his mannerliness. Reston added: "That's what I liked about the guy." So did others.

On July 15, 1965, the *New York Times* announced Stevenson's death this way: "To the public dialogue of his time he brought intelligence, civility, and grace. We who have been his contemporaries have been companions of greatness." In revisiting that announcement, writer Tom Murse adds: "Stevenson is, of course, frequently remembered for his two failed bids for president. But he also left a legacy as an effective and polished statesman" (Murse 8). As the most recent Democratic National Convention

(August, 2024) was unfolding in Chicago, retired journalist Calvin Fentress recalled the 1952 convention, also in Chicago, where he was a fourteen-year-old copy boy for the *Chicago Sun-Times*. Wrote Fentress: "Ahead for Stevenson lay bruising defeats in a life of honor and high purpose. That night in Chicago, he sparked in me, in millions, a flame of idealism, and even here in the political sewer we all now inhabit, it never quite goes out" (Fentress 3). For many reasons, Adlai Stevenson still matters.

American Intellectuals and the Presidency

Abstract Chapter 2 evaluates the definition and uses of the term "intellectual," and explores the dilemmas faced by intellectuals when they become politically engaged. It also contrasts the public and private reaction to intellectuals in politics in the United States with that in many other countries.

Keywords Literary • Liberal • Idealism • Intelligentsia • "highbrow"

> *We find you a speaker indeed, but as it were a soliloquizer on the eternal mountaintops only, in vast solitudes where men and their affairs lie all hushed in a very dim remoteness.*
> —Carlyle to Emerson (Brooks 23)

What is it about American intellectuals, including creative writers, which makes their deliberation about becoming politically active so strained? Is it some sort of cultural dicta peculiar to the United States? Is it something in the personal make-up of intellectuals who live and work in this country? And finally, is there something unique about those candidates they eventually support? As clear as these questions may seem, the answers to them are complex.

© The Author(s), under exclusive license to Springer Nature
Switzerland AG 2025
C. B. Bultman, *Adlai E. Stevenson and American Intellectuals*,
https://doi.org/10.1007/978-3-031-80648-3_2

9

The complexity is framed by several issues raised in this chapter. First is the confusion over what "intellectual" actually means. Second, and closely related, is the problem of accurately applying any agreed-upon definition. Are intellectuals, for example, defined solely by their political stance, in many cases Leftist? Or, on the other hand, are intellectuals more clearly defined by certain qualities of the mind that go beyond political ideologies? The numerous contributing sources to this section of this book express those tensions. Third, intellectuals in the United States have a frequently faced suspicion by the generally non-intellectual public, a suspicion heightened when intellectuals act politically. Fourth, such suspicions are not universally held. That is, intellectuals in many other countries are readily accepted in public positions. Stevenson once quipped in a speech at Oxford University: "The trouble with me is that I always run on the wrong continent" (Cook 134). And fifth, many American intellectuals rallied around Adlai Stevenson even though they admitted that he was not, when defined according to some popular uses of the term, an intellectual.

By virtue of its many uses (and misuses) the very term "intellectual" can be problematic or, at the very least, confusing. Adding to the confusion is that the term is both proudly and pejoratively used in our culture. Dictionaries seem to agree that an intellectual is an intelligent or learned person who shows the ability to think, know, and reason. American historian Richard Hofstadter provides a distinction between one who possesses intelligence and one who possesses intellect. "Intelligence," writes Hofstadter "is excellence of mind, employed within a narrow, immediate, and predictable range," whereas intellect supposes a "critical, creative and contemplative side of the mind" (Hofstadter 25). Klaus Mehnert, a German political scientist, adds that an intellectual need not be an "educated person" in the strict sense of being "learned." He writes that "an intellectual is one who is primarily occupied with three principles: the search for truth, the dedication to humanism, and the struggle for liberty" (Mehnert 91). What can be appreciated about both Hofstadter's and Mehnert's definitions is that both scholars allow for a fusing of two groups which are often treated as disparate. The reference here is to the "literary intellectuals" and the "literary artists," or creative writers. This study uses the term "intellectual" to include both groups. Doing so allows one to treat figures as diverse as Edmund Wilson and John Steinbeck, or Irving Howe and Archibald MacLeish, within the context of political behavior.

To be clearer, the term "intellectual," as used throughout these pages, is not limited to the rather small number of original thinkers in any society, namely, the professional scientists, philosophers, theologians, and other scholars, but includes creative literary artists as well. Furthermore, using the term "intellectuals" in reference to supporters of Adlai Stevenson does not imply that all intellectuals rallied to his candidacy; some, of course, did not.

Adlai E. Stevenson II, the principal of this research, was fond of this more inclusive view of the "educated person," accepting the unity of reason and imagination. Speaking to the 1958 graduates at Michigan State University, Stevenson exhorted: "You have the advantage of education; it is therefore your right and privilege to sustain the sovereignty of intelligence and imagination against the assaults of stupidity and vulgarity" (220). Note that he emphasizes the sovereignty of intelligence (academic intellectuals) *and* imagination (literary intellectuals or creative writers), in the pursuit of a truly worthwhile education. When Stevenson received an honorary degree from Jesus College, Oxford University, in May of 1957, the presenter, Dr. John Traill Christie said, "I present to you for the degree of Doctor of Civil Law, Adlai Stevenson, amid the strains and stresses of national and international politics, the champion of word *and* deed" (Johnson 7: 7). Affirmed that day in Oxford was the international recognition that in championing both acuity in language *and* the importance of action, Stevenson was a distinctive figure among intellectuals.

Even so, lexical problems persist. A brief look at the many uses of "intellectual" may help to show the difficulty in finally arriving at a suitable definition. It seems, for example, that in the realm of politics no agreed-upon definition of intellectual exists. In the history of the Soviet Union, it at one time meant "anti-Czarist," largely because of a section of the university-educated youth who, as "critical thinkers," challenged the established order. At one point in British society, it referred to the "Establishment;" and in Germany it was used on occasion to mean "anti-Nazi." Thus, not only does it appear to have had different meanings from time to time in various countries, but it has also meant different things to people within the same society (Brogan 62). Some believe the term itself came into current use at the time of the Dreyfus Affair in France in 1900. The so-called "intellectuals," also known as the Dreyfusards, were the people who defended Alfred Dreyfus on both moral and intellectual grounds.

> Scientists, historians, and philosophers...they were supposed, on the one hand to be above party battle, and on the other, to be capable, because of their training, of distinguishing the true from the false without being blinded by political or religious passion. (62)

By many accounts it was the novelist Emile Zola who served as the inspiration for the acquittal of Captain Dreyfus, consequently playing a major role in the strengthening of the republic by acting publicly (62).

According to the iconic conservative thinker Russell Kirk, "intellectual" is originally a Marxist word that first appeared in Europe in the nineteenth century ("Eggheads: Cracking the Enigma" 53). The association of intellectualism with the ideas of Marx appears to have been a reason for many Americans to distrust any politicians who have been labeled as "Intellectual." The term, however, contrary to popular belief, is certainly not peculiar to recent history. As noted in the *Oxford Dictionary of The English Language*, "intellectual" was used as early as the Fourteenth Century.

Critics of American intellectuals are likely to refer to them disparagingly as "eggheads," "double-domes," and "highbrows." According to one source, the columnists Joseph and Stewart Alsop are credited with coining the word "egghead" to describe Adlai Stevenson and his followers during the Presidential campaign of 1952. At that time there was speculation that the term was in reference to Stevenson's baldness (Martin 640)! In reality, it was Stewart Alsop who gave birth to the term when he quoted a Republican from Connecticut as saying, "Sure, all the eggheads are for Stevenson. But how many eggheads do you think there are?" ("Whose Adlai?" 32). The term quickly worked its way into general circulation. During that same campaign Dwight Eisenhower offered his own definition. "An intellectual," said Ike, "is a man who takes more words than is necessary to say more than he knows" (Manchester 40). Historian Michael J. Brown recounts a reader's 1957 letter to the *Washington Post & Times*, in which she wrote: "'egghead' has been used in describing many people of great ability—one was Adlai Stevenson. Please call these illustrious people intellectuals, highbrow, or something else denoting their ability—not "'egghead'" (Brown 3).

Many critics feel that intellectuals may be characterized more justly as cultural elitists—persons who are highly educated and cultivated, and who believe that conscious reasoning with intelligence originates only with themselves. Writing in *The Christian Century*, in November of 1952, American journalist Robert Fitch claimed that "Representatives of this class may be found anywhere, but they tend to be numerous among professional people, and they are most class-conscious and articulate among writers and in university faculties (Fitch 1377).

Many of our founding fathers, such as Hamilton, Jefferson, or Madison, would inevitably be referred to as "eggheads" today. In fact, most of them had a healthy respect for intellect. "Even Washington, a supreme embodiment of practical wisdom, could tackle an abstract idea when he chose to do so, and express himself in clear, well-ordered prose" (Brock 70). The most stubborn political egghead of the early constitutional period was probably John Quincy Adams, President from 1825–1829.

Adams had been Professor of Rhetoric at Harvard where he authored *Lectures on Rhetoric and Oratory*. He provided the classic example of the intellectual's alleged inability to communicate to "the masses." On one occasion when he was persuaded to stop in Baltimore on a political speech-making tour, Adams confused the crowd with classical allusions and trilingual puns ("Eggheads: Cracking The Enigma" 54). On another occasion he offered a toast quoting Voltaire "that was so obscure that it confounded even the most sophisticated of observers" (Tulis 73). In the years following John Quincy Adam's Presidency, participation of intellectuals in American politics declined, particularly as Presidential candidates. The man of immediate practical solutions became more influential. Andrew Jackson, for example, followed John Quincy Adams to the White House and ushered in "the age of the common man." Jackson had gained his public stature as a General, and as a man of the people, rather than as a well-educated philosopher. Presidential scholar Thomas Bailey wrote that Jackson was the only President to believe that the earth was not spherical (Bailey 137).

Though Abraham Lincoln is viewed as a writer of distinction, he was also student of great literature, particularly the works of William Shakespeare, George Gordon Byron, and Robert Burns. After Lincoln, the first evidence that intellectuals were once again striving for high political office, and the Presidency directly, came early in the twentieth century with the appearance of Theodore Roosevelt and Woodrow Wilson.

Roosevelt's Harvard background, which included Phi Beta Kappa honors, his authorship of significant historical works such as *The Naval War of 1812* (1882), biographies of Thomas Hart Benton and Gouverneur Morris, and *The Winning of The West*, a four-volume tome, written while in his twenties and thirties, and his connection to the journalistic-literary world through his friendships with well-known muckrakers Upton Sinclair and Jacob Riis, all encouraged his acceptance as an intellectual.

Wilson's Princeton background, his doctorate in political science from Johns Hopkins University, his roles as college professor (Bryn Mawr and Wesleyan) and university president (Princeton) placed him in good stead with intellectuals. His books *Congressional Government* in 1885, *Division and Reunion* in 1893, *George Washington* in 1895 and *A History of the American People*, a five-volume work in 1902, surely helped his stature in intellectual circles. The Wilson Presidency, however, may give us a glimpse of a growing incompatibility between the demands of high political office and the normal accouterments of an intellectual life. By the time he left the Princeton presidency to become Governor of New Jersey in 1910, and through the years in Washington, Wilson did not continue to read and write widely, admitting at one point that he had not read a serious book in fourteen years ("Eggheads" 54).

Despite the example of Wilson's apparent sacrifice of his own intellectual pursuits to political realities, both Theodore Roosevelt and Woodrow Wilson initially elicited the accolades of the American intelligentsia. In 1902 some members of the National Institute of Arts and Letters (including Edmund Clarence Stedman, the poet, Edward MacDowell, the composer, and Robert Underwood, assistant editor of *Century* magazine) called for a newer, smaller, and more exalted body. Their suggestion gave birth to the fifty-member National Academy of Arts and Letters, which counted both Roosevelt and Wilson among its new and very exclusive membership (Cowley, *Writer's Trade* 161).

In the 1930s and 1940s intellectuals rose to great heights as ranking political figures of Franklin Roosevelt's New Deal. They were everywhere and everywhere exceedingly visible. The original "brains trust" included Columbia professors Raymond Moley, Adolphe Berle, and Rexford Tugwell, but grew rather quickly to encompass creative writers such as Archibald MacLeish, Robert Sherwood, and John Steinbeck. These individuals advanced speedily from positions as memorandum writers to policy planners and developers. Their direct relationships with professional politicians, however, were often strained. Congressman Maury Maverick of Texas recalled the frustration in dealing with Tugwell:

> He used professorial language and said something about "averting a revolution." I was going blind. Then, to prove his point, he said: "And the workers and farmers, combining their genius (and another word I couldn't get), and they shall form a nodule." I blew up completely. I said, "Rex, I am sore and insulted, and do not want to hear anymore."
>
> "Why?" he asked. "What in God's name is a nodule?" I said. "A nodule is..." began Rex.
>
> "Stop! Stop!" I shouted. "Don't tell me. Whenever you use a word that I don't understand, it makes me mad. I am an American! The word nodule is not understood by the American people, nor is understood by me, which makes it worse...Nodule my eye! Put your speech in simple language. I never heard of a nodule before. Besides, it sounds like sex perversion." (Anderson 33)

Maverick's comments exhibit an opposition to Tugwell's rhetoric which was cultural rather than ideological. Like Maverick, Lyndon Baines Johnson would later struggle to connect with ideological associates who were culturally removed from Texas progressivism. The opinion of Maverick and others like him notwithstanding, such was the general acceptance of the role played by this new "Washington cognoscenti" in the center of national power that it was suddenly not inconceivable that someone with a reputation as an intellectual could someday return to the Presidency. But the rise in the brains trust was a mixed blessing for intellectuals. Some of them faced objections because they were Easterners, some because they were over-educated elitists, still others because they were identified with left-wing politics. Highly educated scientists accused of selling atomic secrets to the enemy, and especially the trial (1949) and retrial (1950) of Alger Hiss did not endear intellectuals to mainstream Americans. Hiss fit perfectly the prevailing perception; he was an Eastern, Ivy League elitist and predictably perfidious. In many minds "intellectual" and "communist" became synonymous, and an even greater-than-normal wave of anti-intellectualism swept the country.

In 1952, with McCarthyism intensifying, Pulitzer Prize winning novelist Lewis Bromfield, described by William Manchester as an anti-intellectual intellectual, defined an intellectual as

> a person of intellectual pretensions, often a professor or a protégé of a professor, superficial in approach to any problem, feminine, supercilious, filled with conceit, a doctrinaire supporter of middle European socialism, self-righteous and a bleeding heart. (Manchester 766)

In the middle of the next decade, President Lyndon B. Johnson passed similar judgment. "I am not going to have anything to do with liberals," said Johnson, "They won't have anything to do with me. They all follow the communist line...liberals, intellectuals, communists. They're all the same" (Goodwin 392). That Johnson really meant what he said is doubtful. He had had the support of liberals and intellectuals on legislative matters important to all of them: Civil Rights and The Great Society. What is clear from Johnson's statement is that he had become increasingly aggravated by intellectuals' rejection of him. He had provided the political leadership necessary for the legislative success of the Civil Rights Act of 1964, the Voting Rights Act of 1965 and the myriad anti-poverty programs, actions dear to the hearts of many intellectuals. After doing much to win them over, he felt they had turned on him. Adlai Stevenson? Yes. John Kennedy? Yes. Lyndon Johnson? No. Intellectuals' repudiation of him led Johnson to adopt publicly the belief he had probably always felt privately, that they were pompous, self-serving, and self-righteous. John Brademas, long-time congressman, and past president of New York University, noted that "both President Kennedy and President Johnson profited greatly from Stevenson's link with the intellectual and university communities in the country" (Liebling 184).

So it was that in the late 1940s and beyond that just about any intellectual politician, and even those who appeared to be intellectual, were criticized for carrying an air of self-righteousness that repulsed everyone except the intellectuals themselves. Three weeks after the election in 1952, Robert Fitch wrote that the intellectuals' self-righteousness

> is apt to be most virulent in two classes...the clergy and the learned professions: in the first, because it claims to be the guardian of morality; in the second because it claims to be the guardian of truth. The intelligentsia, which includes both as subclasses, is therefore, well-freighted with self-righteousness. (Fitch 1378)

Twenty-five years after Fitch's comment, economist John Kenneth Galbraith, himself an intellectual, provided a slightly different slant in offering that "intellectuals have usually thought themselves disliked because others were jealous of their brains. More often it is because they make trouble" (Galbraith 197).

Whether the mistrust of intellectuals is the result of the association of the word "intellectual" with Marxist ideas, as was especially prevalent during the McCarthy era; the cultural barrier between the general population and the intellectual community, as expressed by the exasperated Maury Maverick; the flaunted self-righteousness of the intellectual, as viewed by the disgruntled LBJ; or simply because "they make trouble," as indicated by Galbraith, is open to debate.

Without question, such suspicions about intellectuals have frequently dimmed the chances for "one of their own" to occupy the White House. This has not meant, however, that American intellectuals automatically, and with regularity, assume an apolitical posture. As was noted earlier, intellectuals have often been advisors to national office holders; Roosevelt's brains trust in the 1930s and Kennedy's in the early 1960s provide excellent examples. Some intellectuals have played the role of "weather makers" (Klaus Meinert's term) who feel and anticipate political currents and shape the future by writing analyses and interpretation (Meinert 93). The group of interest here, however, is the intellectuals, especially literary intellectuals, who actually take positions on political issues, and who really seek to directly influence public debate. This group of intellectuals is considerably smaller in number than those who take indirect approaches. Why so small a group? Is it because in the United States intellectuals find it easier to "retire into a protective shell of irony" (Macdonald 23) than to risk becoming part of the political establishment? William Brock, professor of history at Glasgow University, Scotland, seems to support such a conclusion. He writes:

> In many countries intellectuals have a close interest in politics but find it difficult to bring their influence to bear upon political decisions. *This is particularly true in the United States* [emphasis mine] where intellectuals have often been acutely sensitive to their exclusion from the centers of power, while practical politicians are frequently contemptuous of idealists and exploit the popular distrust of men who claim superior knowledge. Indeed, alienated intellectuals and anti-intellectual public men have become familiar stereotypes. (Brock 69)

Brock is correct on this. In other parts of the world intellectuals are not only accepted as an integral part of political discourse, but are often entrusted with the highest public positions. Examples from the first half of this century are numerous, but one immediately thinks of the novelist and critic Andre Malraux, who served both as Minister of Cultural Affairs and Minister of Information in France, and influential writer Nikos Kazantzakis, who served in a variety of official government positions between 1919 and 1947 in Greece. Taking seriously Albert Camus's warning that silence has dangerous implications, Kazantzakis encouraged intellectuals' political involvement, writing that "The writer cannot repress his indignation nor shirk his responsibility" (Bien 156). And Jean-Paul Sartre "maintained that literature for its own sake is a bourgeoise luxury, that writers must engage, *must* engage with the world" (Bakekwell 322). The idea of *literature engagee* swayed American expatriate, journalist Janet Flanner to pen an essay explaining why she was shifting her interest from art to politics, writing that "The arts are peace products.... Certainly, when men are frightened of having their bodies dismembered in a war is no moment to inquire...' Are you still fond of Picasso's blue period, or do you think Proust's works so bourgeoise that they cannot survive?'" (Weiss 219).

Irish poet Seamus Heaney wrestled with this dilemma in much the same way when considering what he should do in response to "The Troubles." In a review of *The Letters of Seamus Heany* (2024), Maggie Doherty writes that he "also recognized that to be the kind of poet he wanted to be—what he called a public poet, like Robert Lowell or W.B. Yeats—he would have to respond to the circumstances in which he found himself. The public poet concerned himself with the polis and its problems" (Doherty 63).

The novelist, poet and dramatist Gunter Grass, whose political participation is probably unequaled among German writers, in a 1966 interview for *Le Monde*, issued a strong condemnation of "intellectuals who only publish manifestoes. You don't change anything that way. If you want to change something, you have to work very hard at specific things" (Yates 215). This presumably meant that intellectuals ought to move from political literature to political activism through which they become players rather than mere chroniclers and ideological theorists. Grass became a confidant of German Chancellor Willy Brandt.

In the last two decades of the twentieth century and the first two of the twentieth-first, direct political involvement by intellectuals continues to appear more readily accepted abroad than here in the United States. In Peru, Mario Vargas-Llosa, a novelist, narrowly missed being elected president in 1990. In Hungary, Arpad Goncz, also a novelist, as well as a translator, was elected that country's first President selected without Soviet interference. Goncz was once condemned to life imprisonment for his role in the 1956 uprising. In Lithuania, Vytautas Landsburgis, a music professor, served as the first president of an independent Baltic republic.

Landsburgis's grandfather was a playwright exiled to Siberia by the Russian Czar for writing plays in the Lithuanian language. Perhaps the most well-known of these intellectual-presidents, dissident playwright Vaclav Havel of the Czech Republic, received an enthusiastic reception in the Congress of the United States during a state visit. Here, ironically, in the halls of official power, we could applaud the political success of an intellectual elsewhere while maintaining long-standing suspicions toward that same possibility at home.

Like Goncz and Landsbergis, Havel never before held political office. Like Hungarians, and Lithuanians, Czechs did not seem to care. Columnist Rushworth Kidder pointed out at the time (1990) that the notion of Havel as a figure divorced from politics *because* [emphasis mine] he is a literary figure is as lamentably American as it is inaccurate (Kidder 13). He continues:

> In the literature of the English-speaking nations, to be sure, politics is simply one subject among many. In many other cultures, however, politics is *the* subject, the whetstone upon which every major writer sharpens his or her greatness. (13)

John Seigenthaler, Chairman Emeritus of *The Nashville Tennessean*, returned from a June, 1992, trip to Prague with the comment that Havel "is gracious and eloquent" and "would be totally out of place in New York this week" (the week of the Democratic National Convention, July 1992) (Lamb, July 22, 1992). In his country, Havel could be accepted publicly while saying he would lead through "the special radioactive power of the truthful word" (Kidder 13). It is difficult to imagine hearing such phrasing from any candidate during the most recent Presidential race in the United States. Havel noted "the warning voices of poets must be carefully listened to, and taken very seriously...perhaps even more seriously than the voices of bankers or stockbrokers" (Havel 2).

Kidder believes that Havel, and surely others as well, cannot be judged by American standards. Here in the United States these men would be noted as "just writers," as "mere writers." Or worse, they would be miscast altogether. Such miscasting is rarer in Europe, though Havel, whom fellow playwright Arthur Miller called "the world's first surrealist president," admitted that some intellectuals in Czechoslovakia considered him their "ambassador or spy in the world of the political establishment." He feared that politicians would view him "as an alien element" and as "an amateur or dreamer who forced himself upon their community." What the would-be philosopher-king and leader of the "Velvet Revolution of 1989" found instead, was just the opposite. Said Havel in 1991: "I get along with politicians very well and they take my presence as refreshing" (*Newsweek* 31). Vargas Llosa, too, found national power invigorating and chose to title his memoir of 1993 *A Fish in the Water*. Yet, Havel remained especially disappointed with Western academics in whom he discerned the "fraudulence" of their "interpassive nature," essentially "disinterested in activity" except when it could be used to fuel their ideological dreams (Zizek 14). A second revolution, less soft than the one he led, dissolved the tenuous unity of Czechs and Slovaks. No one has suggested that Havel's intellectual nature either spawned or accelerated these dramatic changes. The current and continuous eruptions of nationalism in Eastern and Southern Europe have deposed long-standing politicos just as decisively.

On occasions when someone runs for the American Presidency who is appealing to intellectuals, or when intellectuals adopt an issue of the day, the debate over the extent to which they should participate politically intensifies. In the 1960s, when many intellectuals felt pressed to respond to civil rights issues and the war in Vietnam, W.H. Auden, an American citizen since 1939, could not imagine why anyone would seek the opinion of writers on controversial political issues. He remarked:

> Their views have no more authority than those of any reasonably well-educated citizen. Indeed, when read in bulk, the statements made by writers, including the greatest, would seem to indicate that literary talent and political common sense are rarely found together. (Gass 16)

In his eulogy for William Butler Yeats, who once actually held political office, Auden lamented that "poetry makes nothing happen" (Kidder 13).

Auden, of course, had not always felt so strongly about the division of literature and politics. During the 1930s, he was influenced by a preoccupation with Marx and Freud and an association with left-wing writers such as Stephen Spender and Christopher Isherwood, a preoccupation, and association that compelled Auden to serve in the Spanish Civil War as a stretcher bearer for the Republicans.

Auden was not the only important writer identified with causes to eventually feel a gap necessary between art and politics. Katherine Anne Porter argued that

All working, practical political systems, even those professing to originate in moral grandeur, are based upon and operate by contempt of human life and individual fate; in accepting any one of them and shaping his mind and work to that mold, the artist dehumanizes, unfits himself for the practice of any art. (Aldrich xiii)

American-born T.S. Eliot carried this attitude with him to the shores of Britain, arguing against "the meddling of men of letters in practical affairs" (Panichas xxx). Like Auden and Porter, Eliot feared such meddling would impose political ideology on art. Numerous, indeed, are the voices who find a natural enmity between political values and literary values.

Some American intellectuals, however, have neither assumed nor accepted the divorce of art and politics. Malcolm Cowley, for example, was "convinced that literature and politics, art, science, and education, are all departments of life, and no artist or writer can divest himself of his role in life" (Cowley, "Revolutionary Critic" 202). He emphasized this point in a letter to critic and philosopher, Kenneth Burke: "We are not critics or short-story writers; we are poets: in other words, we are interested in every form of human activity" ("Exile's Return" 221).

But even Cowley was at least suspicious of intellectuals in power. In a 1940 letter to Edmund Wilson, he wondered "what the world would be like if it were run by intellectuals. Some of them we know are admirable people, humble and conscientious, but intellectuals in the mass are not like that. A world run by them would be a very unpleasant place" (*Writer's Trade* 156). Later on in the letter, Cowley tried to clarify his view for Burke, and probably for himself as well. He continued:

Note that nothing I said about the intellectuals is to be construed as an attack on the *intelligence* [emphasis mine], which remains our best and almost our only tool for making this country a better place to live in. I am thinking of the intellectuals as a class...which compare pretty unfavorably with the folkways of coal miners and dairy farmers. (156)

Inherent in Cowley's comments is a pervasive paradox. American intellectuals find it very difficult to reconcile their art with activist politics. The intellectual wants to be influential and accepted, but not *too* influential and not *too* accepted. Writing for the *New Republic* in the early thirties, historian Benjamin Ginzburg saw it this way:

In no other country of the world is there such a tremendous gap between the values recognized by intellectuals and the values that actually govern political and economic realities. And yet, in no other country is the intellectual so preoccupied with affecting the course of politics to the exclusion of his intellectual interests. The less power he has of determining conditions, the more passionate, it would seem, is his will-o-the-wisp quest for political influence. (Ginzburg, 16)

Here again is the paradox. By carrying his values, primarily the value of self as a disinterested searcher for truth, into the political arena, the intellectual stands to gain respectability, but at the same time he loses the legitimacy of his craft. Noted cultural critic Van Wyck Brooks observed that the American tradition of "getting things done, of definite accomplishment" really forces intellectuals into this trap. In his view, "the natural temper of the country is horribly evangelical" and that the intellectual feels that he has achieved respectability "only when he is trying to get some new idea across" (Brooks 54). In other words, the culture of the United State mandates that to be worthwhile one needs to show results. It is not enough to be contemplative, reflective, and thoughtful. What really matters in such a culture is the willingness of the intellectuals to sacrifice artistic ambition for the good of humanity. Novelist William Saroyan, for example, believed that art and politics must come closer together; that "reflection and action must be equally valid in good men." "The weakness of art," he wrote, "is that poems do not ennoble politics as they should, and the trouble with politics is that they inspire poets only to mockery and scorn.... This kind of isolation of entities, while convenient, is, I believe, foolish" (Saroyan 133).

More forcefully, Saroyan added, "Art is answerable to politics and politics is answerable to art, and both are answerable to man, so that when there is disgrace in life...we are all guilty" (133).

Thus, "a certain amount of schizophrenia among intellectuals is understandable" (Berman 21). How can intellectuals "confirm their status without eroding their function? How can they acquire prestige and status in the eyes of the public without being converted into technicians pinned by the vice of process and bureaucracy?" (13).

Cultural critic Robert Brustein's answer is that in America they cannot. Brustein, angered at the government for using the artist and his art for political purposes, argues that the greatest threat to intellectuals

> is the temptation to power and influence and I have no faith whatever in the artist-politician. For a while the artist may bring a sense of style to politics. He brings, I am afraid, no superior wisdom. Quite the contrary, his politics is often a frightening blend of lunacy and demagoguery, while his art...and this is worse...becomes an instrument of his power drive rather than of his imagination. (Brustein 161)

Also a respected cultural critic, Philip Rahv expressed a slightly more tolerant, yet troubled, view than Brustein in writing that politics was neither good nor bad for the writer. But like so many others, Rahv was intentional in focusing on the specific questions of what the artist is actually doing in politics, asking in *The Partisan Review* in 1939: "What is he doing with it [politics] and what is it doing to him? How does his political faith affect him as a craftsman, what influence does it exercise on the moral qualities and on the sensibility of his work" (Aaron 392)? These questions are not new. They were visited by the ancients and have been raised as a matter of intellectual discourse ever since. In British novelist Graham Greene's, *The End of The Affair* a character says: "Faith kills art. To have some faith in anything but the efficacy of art is a sin against art, and the artist pays a terrible price for such sins."

Yet, Archibald MacLeish remained hopeful, writing in a 1953 essay "The Muses' Sterner Laws," that "Loyalty to the art of poetry cannot be taken to justify a rejection of the human world of tragedy and choice. On the contrary, it is precisely loyalty to the art of poetry which most ineluctably imposes the acceptance of the modern world" (MacLeish 172). His position was even more clearly stated in "The Isolation of the American Artist," an essay written in 1958. He offered that "The nature of art is action, and there is not a part of human experience, public or private, on which it cannot act or should not" (186).

Despite the suspicions and warnings of many in their ranks, intellectuals have occasionally "joined the clamor below;" sometimes as candidates for public office themselves, but more often as supporters of politicians who are deemed acceptable. One of those "acceptable," and one who received an inordinate number of endorsements from the intelligentsia, was Adlai Ewing Stevenson II, one term Governor of Illinois and the Democratic presidential nominee in 1952 and 1956. Why Stevenson? And why not Dwight Eisenhower instead? After all, at the time (1948–1952), Eisenhower was an apolitical president of an Ivy League university (Columbia), while Stevenson had become Governor of Illinois largely because of skillfully playing the game designed by machine politicians. In fact, one Stevenson biographer points out that according to the standards of the intelligentsia "he [Stevenson] was not bookish or learned enough" more political than theoretical, "never an innocent among wolves" (Muller 3). Harry Truman disagreed saying that "Stevenson won't listen to the pros; he just goes on with his fancy talk" (Cooke 145).

Why risk further schizophrenia? Was he worth the risk because they thought that he was one of them? Numerous reasons have been offered for the intellectuals' affinity for Stevenson, a posture often described as being "madly for Adlai." He was seen as a "highly literate man, at home in the world of ideas, at ease in the company of intellectuals...he talked like one" (3). He also revealed a literary quality through eloquent speeches and wonderfully crafted prose.

As frequently cited is the view that Stevenson was "just like them": ambivalent, reluctant, witty, cultured, cynical, yet idealistic. Another claim puts their heightened enthusiasm for Stevenson as a reaction to their lack of political vitality; he was able to do what they themselves could not jus-tify, nor legitimize. Intellectuals knew, as surely as Stevenson did, that he could never be fully "one of them." At the same time, he did carry many of their qualities into the political arena and if, in the end, no definition of intellectual is broad enough to include Stevenson, at the very least he became the symbol of one, exuding the airs of an intellectual – the form rather than substance.

It would be a mistake to attribute the intellectuals' attachment to one particular Stevenson characteristic. On the contrary, a serious assessment will show that the political and intellectual support for his candidacies is laced with the kind of ambiguity that exists in the way that the general population feels about intellectuals and how intellectuals feel about themselves. Intellectuals often criticize those they view as anti-intellectuals for not tolerating ambiguity, but when it comes to political action, they seem to have little toleration for it themselves.

Interest in the case of Adlai Stevenson and American intellectuals is fueled by such complexities. The relationship shows, however, that for whatever assemblage of reasons, Stevenson brought the affairs of men and women, returning to Carlyle's admonition of Emerson, from a "hushed" and "very dim remoteness" to a point where intellectuals left their "vast solitudes" on "eternal mountaintops" to participate in presidential politics.

Stevenson arriving in Chicago for the Democratic National Convention, 1952

Adlai Stevenson and American Intellectuals

Abstract Chapter 3 addresses Stevenson's own intellectual development and his relationship with the American intellectual community at large, and especially with literary intellectuals

Keywords Ideology • Civil rights • Conservative • Anti-intellectual

> *And "When the prince has gathered about him*
> *All the savants and artists, his riches will be fully employed."*
> —Ezra Pound *Pound, Ezra* (Canto XIII)

The literary and cultural critic Edmund Wilson recalled making passionate love to his wife, Elena, as they listened to an Adlai Stevenson speech on the radio. "I said afterward," wrote Wilson in his memoir on the fifties, "that this had been an ideal way to listen to a campaign speech, and she said that if everyone could have heard Stevenson like that, he would be overwhelmingly elected" (Wilson 397).

Although the Wilsons apparently would never forget him, Adlai E. Stevenson II is already removed by time from common and quick identification by millions of Americans. Most who recall his quests for the Presidency in 1952 and 1956 recognize that despite losing the elections,

C. B. Bultman, *Adlai E. Stevenson and American Intellectuals*,
https://doi.org/10.1007/978-3-031-80648-3_3

27

and in the case of 1960, the nomination, he was respected even by many of those who voted against him. Among those who voted for him there were particular groups whose attitudes toward him went beyond admiration to reverence, and perhaps even to canonization. Certainly, many of the literary intellectuals of his day developed an affinity for Stevenson which has not been equaled by any presidential candidate since. He had widespread support among the intelligentsia generally, but the special relationship he forged with those in the literary world is the focus of this chapter.

The evidence will show that this relationship was not, in Lionel Trilling's words, the "dark and bloody crossroads where literature and politics meet" (Trilling 22). Rather, it will show that despite differences between the literary-intellectual world and the political world, they were, for one brief, shining (as the principals saw it) moment, woven together by the thread that was Adlai Stevenson.

Although Van Wyck Brooks obviously did not have Adlai Stevenson in mind when writing *America's Coming of Age* in 1915, his terminology works quite well in describing Stevenson's role in bringing many intellectuals into the political arena. Brooks identified "highbrow" and "low-brow" as authentically American terms representing "two currents in the American mind running side by side but never mingling" (Brooks 19). One, the "highbrow," describes a "superior person" of the "desiccated culture;" the other, "the lowbrow," describes "a good fellow" of "stark utility" (18,22). It can be argued that Stevenson, as a politician with intellectual leanings, emerged somewhere between the two. In so doing, he ushered in an occasion on which the "irreconcilable planes" of stark intellectuality and stark business, the planes of "highbrow" and "lowbrow" moved closer. It was one of those rare times when, in Brooks's phrase, there was a "harnessing of thought and action together" (Brooks 31). Incidentally, Brooks describes Woodrow Wilson, the recognized intellectual President, as a "permutation and combination" of these two currents (20), a condition which Brooks found to be natural and not altogether unacceptable.

Legendary satirist H.L. Mencken reportedly once said to the novelist James T. Farrell that the three traps for a writer were alcohol, women, and politics (Martine 311). This chapter opens with the question of why so many writers and critics fell into the "trap of politics" by becoming publicly active in Stevenson's presidential campaigns, and is developed by suggesting several possible answers.

The range of feasible reasons for the intellectuals' support of Adlai Stevenson is wide. Stevenson's perceived liberalism, for example, attracted some intellectuals. So did his cultural and literary heritage. Others were mainly lured by Stevenson's eloquence and wit. Many were fond of his reluctance to assume political power, especially since they rejected his contemporaries for wanting it too much, or for exercising it badly. They appreciated, too, his internationalist-universalist tenor, his emphasis on reason, and his idealism. For many intellectuals the composite Stevenson, that is, a man who was at least thought to possess all of the pre-ceding qualities, was simply irresistible. He might be, they supposed, the path to their cultural and political relevance.

In the overview of these many qualities, political ideology appears to be the weakest bond between intellectuals and the Stevenson candidacies. If one assumes the left-of-center posture for most intellectuals of Stevenson's day, would it not follow that, on the whole, they would have demanded that he fall into their own ideological niche? On the surface, the argument of ideological compatibility is credible. The army of intellectuals who supported Stevenson shared many of his liberal notions about the nature and purpose of government. There seems to have been, for example, a unanimity against the right-wing irrationality of the late 1940s and early 1950s. When Stevenson asked Archibald MacLeish to offer ideas for a speech to be delivered at the 1952 American Legion convention in New York City, MacLeish replied:

> Patriotism is the ideal which holds the Legion together. But it is also the mask behind which some of the most dangerous and evil influences of our day conceal themselves...in the Legion and outside it. The McCarthys and the Jenners: the black listers and subverters of free education. (Winnick 360)

And an article in the *Saturday Review* proclaimed: "Nothing in the fifties damaged the image of the United States more than the excesses of Senator [Joseph] McCarthy; nothing restored it more than the public expressions of Stevenson" (Natwar-Singh 35).

Although MacLeish and the *Saturday Review* do not represent all the intellectuals who supported Stevenson, they do remind us that Stevenson was viewed by many of them as the proper antidote to the kind of intellectual martial law which they thought existed in the late 1940s and early 1950s. He had dared, after all, to go ahead with the Hiss deposition when it was clear that no general political gain was likely. In response to a series of questions from the "Direct Interrogatories in Behalf of Defendant Alger Hiss," Stevenson had simply attested by "Yes" or "No" and "Good" or "Bad" answers to Hiss's reputation for integrity, loyalty, and veracity. During the campaign of 1952, Stevenson would be described by Republican vice-presidential candidate Richard Nixon in a nationally televised speech as "going down the line for the arch-traitor of our generation" (Weinstein 511). Hiss's guilt or innocence aside, intellectuals found appealing Stevenson's willingness to stand up against a witch hunt in which they were often the prey.

At about the same time as the Hiss deposition (1949), then Governor of Illinois, Stevenson courageously vetoed the Broyles Bill, which would have made it a felony to belong to any subversive organization and required that all public employees, as well as candidates for public office, submit to a loyalty oath. His veto message appealed to intellectuals.

> The whole notion of loyalty inquisitions is a natural characteristic of a police state, not of a democracy...The vast majority of our people are intensely loyal, as they have amply demonstrated. To question, even by implication, the loyalty and devotion of a large group of citizens is to create an atmosphere of suspicion and distrust... In conclusion, while I respect the motives and patriotism of the proponents of this bill, I think there is in it more of a danger to the liberties we seek to protect than of security for the Republic. (Martin, *Illinois* 450)

Liberal intellectuals were favorably impressed, too, by Stevenson's support for ending both the draft and hydrogen bomb testing, and for his undying advocacy of the United Nations as a tool to mediate peace, particularly in the Middle East (Davis 345). His progressive views on public service, aid to education, health care, and programs for the elderly also scored points with liberal intellectuals. They paid close attention when

Stevenson pointed out that the Eisenhower administration had forty thousand employees working on the problems concerning businesses, but only nine in the entire Department of Health, Education and Welfare dealing with the difficulties of fourteen million senior citizens (Muller 183).

Still, if one searches for a purely liberal ideologue of the New Deal-Fair Deal traditions, Adlai Stevenson cannot always be found. Stevenson biographer Rodney Sievers has pointed out a pervasive ambiguity: "Like the liberals, he believed that the country should be constantly engaged in reform; like the conservatives, he thought reform should be gradual" (Sievers 114). Arthur M. Schlesinger, Jr. admitted that during Stevenson's campaigns some of his advisors attempted to make him more liberal than he was "to help him overcome his [privileged] upbringing" (Baker 338).

Both Leftist and Rightist critiques deny that he was liberal at all. I.F. Stone's *The Haunted Fifties* (1963) and Paul Carter's *Another Part of The Fifties* (1984), are good examples. On the Left, Stone rails against Stevenson's "soft" positions in foreign and domestic affairs, accusing him of "double talk" (Stone 107, 112). On the Right, Carter agrees with Stone's analysis and adds that Stevenson was noticeably conservative on questions of federal authority. "Americans who had listened for two decades to the New Deal-Fair Deal argument that a humane national government's social activity could bring blessings to all," writes Carter, "were startled" when Stevenson, in his very first campaign speech, condemned "'the increasing centralization of our lives in Washington'" (Carter 14). Although Stevenson was more inclined to talk about states' responsibilities than states' rights, his rhetoric must have given conservatives some comfort. Harry Truman, ever suspicious of Stevenson, said that he [Stevenson] "has always been a conservative, I think he was born that way" (Sievers 113). Stevenson, indeed, was leery of radical changes that went too far, too fast, and when in speeches he used the word "moderation," more liberal friends like Averell Harriman, Hubert Humphrey, and Herbert Lehman vehemently objected (Johnson 6:9).

Stevenson's reluctance to take the lead on civil rights probably frustrated liberal intellectuals as much as any issue by which he was judged. In 1956 Stevenson spoke in favor of a Democratic Party platform that rejected "all proposals for the use of force to interfere with the orderly determination of these matters by the courts" (Stone 112). He did, in fact, oppose using federal troops to accelerate desegregation. He also publicly opposed an amendment to school aid legislation which would have denied federal aid to segregated schools. It did not help that he had accepted John Sparkman, an Alabama segregationist, as his running mate in 1952.

Taylor Branch's massive, three-volume Pulitzer Prize winning study of civil rights from 1954 to 1963 is especially critical of Stevenson's "gradualism." In it Branch recounts the denunciation of Stevenson by most major civil rights leaders because of his "blithe vagueness" on issues of race (Branch 191). Stevenson is described as uncomfortable among blacks, even refusing to talk with Coretta Scott King during negotiations for her husband's release from prison because "it was not proper as he had not been introduced to her" (360). Adam Clayton Powell said that "Negroes who voted for Stevenson were traitors to their race" (Baker 381). During the 1952 campaign, Stevenson refused to change hotels when a black reporter was denied a room asking why the journalist "couldn't go somewhere else" (341). When Emmett Till's mother traveled the country to amplify the injustice behind the murder of her son, Stevenson referred to her tour as "a spectacle" (342). And when Eisenhower received about sixty percent of black votes in 1956, Stevenson lamented: "I am quite bewildered about the Negroes" (Branch 191). As far as civil rights were concerned, liberal intellectuals were among those who were more than a little bewildered about Stevenson.

Stevenson defended himself by citing his support for desegregating some schools and for a Fair Employment Practices Act, both while Governor of Illinois, as well as his effort to desegregate the Navy during World War II (Baker 343). Some intellectuals could appreciate Stevenson's commitment to "reason" on civil rights: "We must recognize that it is reason alone that will determine our rate of progress" (191). Eric Sevareid, a widely respected journalist, for one, was prepared to defend his [Stevenson's] perspective, writing that sometimes "the moderate position requires more courage than the extreme position" (Johnson 6: 64). On this issue, Sevareid and Stevenson seemed to fuel the adage that "a wise man does not try to hurry history." His very good friend Maritta Tree said that "They [Blacks] wanted equality of opportunity and wanted it now. It was hard for him [Stevenson] to understand the urgency" (Adlai Stevenson Project 92).

The point here is that Stevenson's commitment to the progressive liberalism of the post-Roosevelt-Truman era was suspect at times and thus could not have been among the strongest of appeals to many of the intellectuals who supported him. If liberalism was the key attraction to a Presidential candidate, they could have rallied behind several others whole liberal credentials were more ideologically salient than Stevenson's. Henry Wallace, Hubert Humphrey, Estes Kefauver, and Averell Harriman, who political scientist V.O. Key described as the "darling of the liberals" (Key 400), would have been more likely choices. In 1994, political writer Garry Wills, while conceding that Stevenson was progressive, labels him as a *moderate* reformer, at most (Wills 80).

Though they may have preferred that Stevenson identify more intensely with liberal causes, his intellectual friends found in Stevenson something that transcended ideology and political identity. John Steinbeck, in a letter written from Mexico a dozen years before his infatuation with Adlai Stevenson, remarked that "from the simple good Indians on the shore to the invertebrates there is a truer thing than ideologies" (Steinbeck, *Letters* 201). In the case of the relationship between Stevenson and intellectuals, there was indeed a "truer thing." The intellectuals' allegiance clearly was not to a candidate espousing specific ideological tenets.

Even Stevenson's mostly friendly biographers recognized that his conservative streak was not only political, but cultural as well. John Bartlow Martin points out, just as Schlesinger does, that when Stevenson joined the national Democratic establishment in 1952, "he had to abandon conservative ideas he had picked up in Bloomington and Lake Forest. He abandoned them reluctantly" (Martin 643).

Stevenson, for instance, carried with him into adulthood and on to public life, a long-harbored suspicion of Jews. He would win their votes even as he championed a homeland in Palestine, but his rearing in the Midwest and his education at Eastern schools attended chiefly by wealthy Protestants established notions that were hard to shake. Comments he made while in his twenties and thirties, in particular, illustrate the conservative side of his upbringing and background. While on a weekend trip from Princeton to New York City, he described to his sister a Jew he had met who was "like most of his race" (Martin, *Illinois* 70). Similarly, during his year at the Agricultural Adjustment Administration, Stevenson disclosed to his wife that "many of them [Jews] are autocratic," but that

"Frank [General Counsel Jerome N. Frank] has none of the racial characteristics" himself, even though he "brought several other Jews down who...are more racial" (105). Just because these kinds of comments were private, rather than public, Stevenson cannot be excused from the moral blame associated with racial or ethnic prejudice.

A retrospective cultural critique would also fault Stevenson for his less-than-progressive view regarding the "proper" role for women. In his 1955 commencement speech at Smith College entitled "Women, Husbands, and History," Stevenson's rhetoric was filled with admonitions which hardly fit the view that he was a man ahead of his times. Opening the message about a world in crisis, Stevenson said, "I want merely to tell you young ladies that I think there is much you can do about that crisis in the humble role of housewife...which, statistically, is what most of you are going to be whether you like the idea or not and you'll like it!" (Johnson 4: 495). Later in the address, Stevenson assigned the worth of college education for the women of Smith consistent with a culturally conservative viewpoint. He said that "far from the vocation of marriage and motherhood leading you away from the great issues of the day, it brings you back to their very center and places upon you an infinitely deeper and more intimate responsibility than that borne by...those who hit the headlines and make the news" (501).

Both preceding examples, one reflecting sheer prejudice, the other revealing a rather narrow view of the public role to be played by women, strongly suggest that while Stevenson may have grown up valuing high culture, he also exhibited common biases of both that culture and the times in which he lived.

Stevenson biographers have noted the cultivated environment in which he was raised. Bloomington was a town surprisingly sophisticated for a down-state Illinois agricultural community. Some of Stevenson's ancestors had given academic and intellectual pursuits a high priority. His great-grandfather, Lewis Warner Green, was President of Centre College in Danville, Kentucky, in the 1850s. Lewis Green had also been President of Presbyterian Theological Seminary, Hampden-Sydney College in Virginia, and Transylvania College, which later became part of the state university system in Kentucky. Stevenson's great-grandmother, Mary Peachy Fry, was a direct descendent of Joshua Fry, an Oxford University graduate and professor of mathematics at the College of William and Mary (Davis 23).

Jesse Fell, Stevenson's grandfather, donated land for the State Normal School, which became Illinois State University, in what was originally North Bloomington, now Normal, Illinois, and led the fundraising drive to support the new college (23). Fell also helped to organize the Free Congregational Society, forerunner of the Unitarian Church in Bloomington. The society was based on a rational faith in which the honest use of one's mind was "an act of devotion to the Supreme Intelligence" (30). Grandfather Fell's attitudes, in large measure, were transmitted to his grandson. Later, the candidate Stevenson's liberal theology, no doubt, would impress the intellectuals as an expression of toleration and a reflection of their own resistance to narrow-mindedness.

The generational link espousing respect for the nurture and cultivation of the mind rested with Stevenson's mother, Helen Davis Stevenson. The Stevenson home on East Washington Street, as large as it was, had no true living room. Rather, the spacious front room was a library where Helen Stevenson encouraged young Adlai's respect for culture. She "believed in the custom of reading to the children from Greek mythology, the classics in English: Victor Hugo, Nathaniel Hawthorne, Ralph Waldo Emerson, James Fenimore Cooper, and the King James version of the Bible" (Ives 14). His appetite for literature and poetry was formed with William Thackery, Charles Dickens, Sir Walter Scott, the Brontes, and George Eliot among his childhood favorites (Johnson 1: 4). As her children's self-appointed literary guide, Helen Stevenson was an intellectual and cultural protectionist of sorts. On one occasion when her husband brought a copy of *Cosmopolitan* into the home, she insisted that he take it to the bedroom, out of sight of the children, so that they would not be exposed to "such trash" (Dick 282). Not surprisingly, when Stevenson later became Governor and found no library at the Governor's Mansion in Springfield, he converted the sunporch into one and began forming a permanent collection (Severn 98).

Despite such a background, Adlai Stevenson "manifested no artistic or literary genius," notes biographer Kenneth Davis. "He was not a brilliant scholar...Far from being intellectually precocious, he seemed to lag behind most of his contemporaries at school in his mental development" (Davis 42). Stevenson's grades at University High School in Bloomington, indeed, were not outstanding. A sampling of his performance in his freshman and sophomore years shows mediocre grades, (mid-70s out of 100 in algebra, zoology, and English), though by the following year he was a much-improved student, pushing his scores (mid-80s and low-90s in all courses) (52).

Even with encouraging academic progress, Stevenson's plan to attend Princeton University had to be put on hold. In 1916, he took the three college entrance examinations required by Princeton and failed them all. Still determined to make it at a reputable university, he enrolled at the Choate preparatory school in Connecticut, but only after making up a French language deficiency (55).

Stevenson admitted later that at Princeton, his "greatest preoccupation was with extracurricular activities" and that he was "content with what we generally called a 'gentleman's third group'" (71). Stevenson biographers agree that his academic achievements were minimal. Herbert Muller writes that Stevenson "was no little egghead and displayed no exceptional interests or abilities" (Muller 18).

Even though Stevenson exhibited no passion for scholarship throughout his academic training at superior institutions (Choate, Princeton, Harvard Law, Northwestern Law), he continued to grow intellectually and received the kind of training that would foster relationships with the learned and the creative. Because his principal interests were the humanities, and because of his liberal religious instruction, he was spared much intolerance.

If there was no passion for scholarship, then in its place was an immense respect for books and the people who wrote them. Clearly, the magnitude of this respect was grounded in the view that writers were very much the caretakers of language and in his equally great respect for ideas, even if they were not his own. The respect for wisdom as expressed in words that began in the family library in Bloomington continued throughout his life. Lest he forget his roots in this regard, there was always the cultivated mother, Helen Stevenson, to remind him. In a 1923 letter to Adlai at Harvard, she continued to emphasize the importance of nurturing relationships with the learned, writing that she was "glad indeed to know you are well and enjoying a rare opportunity…that of really learning. As much as possible, seek the association of wise people…. Don't waste much time on the mediocre. Better to be alone, thinking for yourself" (Ives 169).

A fair extension of Mrs. Stevenson's remarks may be "better to be alone, writing for yourself." Stevenson's critics claim that he has been given far too much credit for writing his own speeches. Biographer John

Bartlow Martin suggests that Stevenson was so adamant about writing his own speeches, and spent so much time doing just that, that he left precious few moments for creative thinking (Martin, *World* 26), and was not really an intellectual "if one considers an intellectual to be one given to creative thinking and interested in ideas for their own sake" (21).

Martin's judgment notwithstanding, Stevenson valued reading, writing, a liberal education, and people with ideas. In one of his three Godkin Lectures at Harvard University, this one in 1954, he voiced, as he would elsewhere, the importance of rigorous thought in shaping a civilized world. He commented:

> The ordeal of our times…is a challenge to American maturity and American responsibility. Nowhere is this testing more fundamental than in the field of the free mind. For never has external threat required more clear-headed analysis, more hard and sober thought, and more bold and unterrified vision than the threat we confront today. And yet the very existence of that threat has created strains and tensions, anguish, and anxiety, which beat upon the free mind, surround it, torment it, and threaten to smother it…. Anti-reason is the spirit of the shouting, chanting crowds we remember so well in Hitler's Germany…. In recent years we have seen the contagion of unreason and anti-intellectualism spreading among ourselves…. America's greatest contribution to human society has not come from her wealth or weapons or ambitions, but from her ideas. (112)

That same year Stevenson was the invited speaker at the senior class banquet at Princeton University. Though largely filled with reminiscences about his days as a Princeton undergraduate and the perfunctory challenges to the soon-to-be graduates, his speech is laced with the recurring theme of the critical need for intellectual growth. "We have bet all our chips, if you please, on the intellectual improvement of our people," said Stevenson. He went on to call this "a magnificent gamble" because it calls into question whether in the United States we have "sufficiently elevated our national mind to lead the world wisely." Continuing, he remarked that "only the educated man entertains doubts, and doubt is the beginning of wisdom; but doubt is not wisdom's fulfillment, and in a time of crisis the man who doubts may fall prey to the strong dumb brute" (Johnson 4: 342).

His concern for the development of the mind, not only for its own sake, but for its use in the betterment of humankind, would be seen as an alluring attribute by many intellectuals. The high-brow *London Economist* wrote that Stevenson was intellectually "the most brilliant Governor" Illinois had had in fifty years (Martin, *Illinois* 382). Presumably, John Peter Altgeld, who was immortalized by Stevenson family friend and poet Vachel Lindsay, was the most recent Illinois governor to receive such praise. Like Stevenson, Altgeld displayed certain intellectual qualities while serving as a social reform-minded state executive. Some intellectuals, however, would be disappointed by Stevenson's mix of intellect and action, perceiving an eventual and inevitable bastardization of critical and creative talent. This latter tension is reflected throughout this study.

Suspicion by some intellectuals aside, Stevenson's academic and cultural heritage helped to create the impression that he was an oasis in a national political desert. Raised in the world of books, liberally educated, accustomed to the company of writers, yet bred and born into a family of political action, he seemed destined to be a rare link between two worlds. He also seemed to fully comprehend the difficulty in such a role. Just before Stevenson's death, journalist Lillian Ross was working on a series of articles about him to be published over several weeks in *The New Yorker*. She accompanied Stevenson through various daily schedules and was given the opportunity to have many conversations with him. In one private moment he told Ross that he "had a taste for literature and academic.... It's been part of the luggage I've carried in public life which doesn't yield public dividends" (Ross 7). More than one observer would credit Stevenson with being witty and erudite but not very good at politics (Gold 23).

Yet, Stevenson relished the role, rarely shunning the label "intellectual" and often promoting it. In 1961 he even commercially encouraged it. White searching for a post-1960 election article about intellectuals' reaction to the young Kennedy presidency, I noticed Stevenson's photograph on the inside cover of the *Saturday Review*. He was pictured in an advertisement for the "Great Books of The Western World" series, and was quoted affirming that the books were "essentials in the library of any thinking person" (*Saturday Review*, May 13, 1961). The self-perception that he was cultured, literate, "a thinking person," and quite willing to be prominently portrayed as such in a respected national magazine of literature and the arts must have contributed to the role he relished. Equally predictable, however, was the possibility that some intellectuals (Dwight Macdonald comes to mind) would wince at Stevenson falling prey to the commercialism of a "middle brow" publication.

The view that Adlai Stevenson respected the power of words, both spoken and written, was assuredly not imaginary. Dr. Eugene Rabinowitch's eulogy of Stevenson in the *Bulletin of the American Scientist* is driven by recollections of a distinctively literate style. He wrote that Stevenson "caught the imagination of intellectuals in America and abroad as a tolerant, rational, humble, and utterly civilized statesman." And after pointing out that the power of words can frequently be used for dishonesty and deceit, Rabinowitch added that "sincere and well-chosen words are the only paths by which ideas can be spread from man to man and from nation to nation.... Men everywhere in the world heard the ring of honesty, intelligence, and good will in the words of Adlai Stevenson" (Rabinowitch 3).

Even at the beginning of his national political career Stevenson's reputation for word-crafting was widespread. *New York Times* columnist James Reston, in reviewing the *Major Campaign Speeches of Adlai Stevenson* in 1953, wrote that among other notable descriptions, "He is first and foremost a philosopher and a writer" (Johnson 5: 202). Perhaps a writer was what he had hoped to be all along. While Stevenson was at Princeton, he was intensely interested in journalism, but hoped that preparation for the business of reporting would eventually lead to a career in creative writing. "He was never quite sure," writes Kenneth Davis, "that what he really wanted to be was a writer" (Davis 78).

In his mid-sixties cultural critique, *Against the American Grain*, Dwight Macdonald laments that "our politicians are still men of narrow culture...whose antipathy to reading is well known" (Macdonald, *American Grain* 396). As was pointed out earlier, Stevenson's reverence for language was well-rooted. In a letter to Davis, he recalled: "As long as I can remember I have read, read, read...anything and everything...at every walking instant...streetcars, taxis, trains, planes,...even elevators and toilets," (Johnson 6: 492). The rigor with which Stevenson pursued clarity of language is also noteworthy. Biographer Davis again: "Something in him...a stubborn integrity, a literary craftsman's respect for words...rebelled against the whole system of ghost-writing and public relations engineering" (Davis 189). At one point Stevenson muttered: "I simply cannot use the conventional banalities of politicians, even if I should" (Baker 33).

His adherence to high standards in the writing of his own speeches is well known. Stevenson not only wanted sound political rhetoric, he demanded that the speeches read and sound like first rate literary pieces. In fact, Stevenson was at his best when preparing texts to be read or heard by others. His personal writing seemed of little importance. When his numerous travel experiences invited writing in a diary, for example, he would begin, only to discontinue after a few days. Among his letters to friends, on the other hand, even the most informal communication sustained his interest and represented a high literary quality. He simply could not write for himself alone.

Stevenson's obsession with his own writing often sparked contentious moments in his political life. Campaign staffers, though immensely respectful of Stevenson the candidate, were often impatient with Stevenson the writer. Last minute changes in speeches sometimes numbered over one hundred (Baker 319). Aide James Finnegan: "Sometimes we'd have to keep our plane in the air…with important local politicians waiting on the ground…while we circled and circled in the sky, while Adlai edited on and on" (Muller 180). Confidant George Ball attested to similar anxiety, not only about Stevenson finishing the writing of speeches on time, but about his seeming inability to complete the delivery of them on time as well. Part of the problem, recalled Ball, was that he "insisted upon inserting additional words, phrases, whole paragraphs at the last minute." On more than one occasion Ball told Stevenson, "You are a fine poet but a lousy architect. You say the right things and say them eloquently, but you don't let the structure of your speeches show through. Consequently, your listeners cannot recall what you've said or that you recommended anything" (Ball 150). On election eve in 1952, Stevenson ran overtime in a televised speech to the nation. Instead of leaving listeners with an eloquent plea for support, the speech trickled off into regular programming (Baker 333). Stevenson's good friend Bill Blair was frequently too upset to watch Stevenson's speeches on television because they would consistently run beyond the allotted time (322).

Ball and other advisors would point out that in contrast, General Eisenhower's speeches were organized by the clear and orderly enumeration of points. Such advice was acknowledged by Stevenson with irritation and resentment. Wrote Ball: "He had a contempt for the pronouncement of obvious points as though a list were a concept, or a litany a program. That was, he felt, a cheap political device and he would have none of it. Besides, it offended his sensibilities as a writer" (150). Even opponent Eisenhower said that he recognized Stevenson's facility for words, but if that were the qualification for the Presidency "we ought to elect Ernest Hemingway" (Larson 15). Ike, by the way, never wanted to see his speeches until he delivered them (Baker 319).

Sometimes Stevenson's literary possessiveness stretched the limits of his obvious civility. William Attwood, with whom Stevenson had a sporadic editorial relationship, in and out of actual presidential campaigns, incurred his wrath over, of all things, words. In the spring of 1960 Stevenson returned to New York from a tour of Latin America, and almost as an addendum to remarks about the trip itself, he was found defending the origin of his speeches. Attwood would later admit to Stevenson's greatness as a writer, even claiming that he himself had become a better writer for having worked with Stevenson; but he had insisted that he had worked to modify Stevenson's "lyrical flashes" and "fine prose," and had even done complete rewrites of some Stevenson pieces (Johnson 5: 319). Fearful that Attwood's public statements would be taken to mean that he (Stevenson) employed "a staff of wordsmiths," Stevenson bristled. As accounts of this appeared in the press, Stevenson at first, with characteristic wit, said, "As for recent newspaper stories about hiring ghost writers, I have suffered from the do-it-yourself habit too long to look or hope for relief now" (7: 450). (Incidentally, ghost writers were hardly new to presidential speech making. Presidential scholar Jeffrey Tulis has reminded students of the office that both James Madison and Alexander Hamilton wrote for George Washington, but that there is a significant difference between that and employing a staff of wordsmiths [Tulis 184].)

Five days after his public comment, Stevenson wrote to Attwood to sever their "editorial relationship because I have two reports…of audible remarks: 'I [Attwood] wrote half the speech; Boyd the other half.…' Frankly, I've never had any experience of this kind before and, even if these reliably reported statements were true, they grossly violate the convention I assumed you knew" (Johnson 7: 462). Eleven days later Stevenson was still troubled by the incident, writing to his dear friend Agnes Meyer that "any such rumors both contradict my political policy and also my literary policy" (474).

A politician with literary policy? The friendly judgment in the Attwood episode is that Stevenson simply had far too much respect for literary quality, particularly his own, to have others write his speeches. Attwood later admitted as much after Stevenson's death, writing: "I doubt if I ever wrote a paragraph for Stevenson that he did not manage to make his own by penciling in some fresh sentence or phrase.... He had such pride of authorship" (Attwood 154). Stevenson never tried to hide that he "used" or "borrowed" phrases from others, and even if others played a role in writing speeches, he surely stamped his own imprimatur on the them (Gold 23). Shortly after Stevenson's death in 1965, a young Illinois Assemblyman and later United State Senator, Paul Simon, wrote that Stevenson "usually won the struggle to make words march to his command" (Simon 136).

Eric Sevareid claimed that the best speech he heard Stevenson give was one delivered on the spur of the moment. In the spring of 1949, Stevenson's neighbor, historian, and friend, Lloyd Lewis died. He began his impromptu remarks at the funeral, saying that

> It is April now and all life is being renewed on the bank of the river he loved so well. We will all be happy that it happened on this day, here by the river with spring sky so clear and the west wind so warm and fresh. I think we will all be better for this day and this meeting together. (Johnson 3: 72)

He concluded with the thought that

> it will always be April in our memory of him. It will always be a bright, fresh day full of infinite variety and the promise of a new life. Perhaps nothing has gone at all...perhaps only embodiment of the thing...tender, precious to all of us...a friendship that is immortal and does not pass along. It will be renewed for me, much as I know it will for all of you, each spring. (72)

Still, it was the public Stevenson whose eloquence enamored so many. His acceptance speech at the Democratic National Convention at Chicago's International Amphitheatre in 1952, was for a great number of intellectuals the event through which they would call him their own. The following excerpt is from that speech:

> I would not seek your nomination for the Presidency because the burdens of that office stagger the imagination. Its potential for good or evil now and in the years of our lives smothers exultation and converts vanity to prayer...Let's tell them [the American people] that the victory to be won in

the twentieth century, this portal to the golden age of man, mocks the pretensions of individual acumen and ingenuity. For it is a citadel guarded by thick walls of ignorance and mistrust which do not fail before the trumpets' blast or the politicians' imprecations. (4:16 and 19)

The response to the speech by those who wrote for a living was overwhelmingly positive. Journalist Mary McGrory, who acclaimed Stevenson's contribution to ideas, language, and courtliness, recalled feeling that "politically speaking, it was the Christmas morning of our lives. Boston born, we [the McGrory family] had never known a poet in politics" (McGrory 170).

Another speech worth noting was one Stevenson delivered in January of 1959. Four thousand people gathered in Constitution Hall in Philadelphia to hear him memorialize the liberal Unitarian minister, A. Powell Davies of All Souls Unitarian Church in Washington, D.C. The speech induced commentary in numerous magazines and the *Saturday Review* published a condensed version the following month. That same month the speech dominated *Life* magazine's editorial under the title "The Cost of Easy Options" (*Life*, February 9, 1959, 31). Stevenson biographer Stuart Gary Brown even devoted an entire chapter to the address in his *Conscience in Politics* (1961). In the speech Stevenson quoted Albert Schweitzer, Goethe, Jean de La Bruyere, the seventeenth-century moralist (in French), Shakespeare, Matthew Arnold, and Abraham Lincoln. His references to them were not thrown in as an indication that he somewhere had a book of famous quotations. Rather, their words and his were woven in a tapestry of moral challenge to his listeners. The following excerpts from "The Political Relevance of Moral Principle" demonstrate the power of the speech.

Today, when the threat and challenge to a free society seem more total and powerful than ever before, it is not a political luxury of fruitless pedantry to re-examine our fundamental principles. I think it more likely to be the condition of survival.

No country on earth owes the sense of community more explicitly to the fact that it is united not by race or nationality but by fidelity to an idea. We were born "dedicated to a proposition" and our greatest leaders...the Jeffersons, the Lincolns, the Woodrow Wilsons...were not great because they achieved purely American purposes, but because they were able to speak for humanity at large and extend their vision to the whole family of man.

He who offers this thing we call freedom as the soft option is a deceiver or himself deceived. He who sells it cheap or offers it as the byproduct of this or that economic system is knave or fool. For freedom demands infinitely more care and devotion than any other political system. It puts consent and personal initiative in the place of command and obedience. By relying upon the devotion and initiative of its citizens, it gives up the harsh but effective disciplines that underpin all the tyrannies which over the millennia have stunted the full stature of man.

Vacuity and indifference are not redeemed by the fact that everyone can share in them. They merely restrict the circle from which regeneration can come.

It has been the view of great philosophers and great statesmen that our system of free government depends in the first instance upon the virtue of its citizens. Montesquieu made virtue the condition of republican government; Washington declared that it could not survive without it.... I believe they are right. For no democratic system can survive without at least a large and active leaven of citizens in whom dedication selflessness are not confined to private life but are the fundamental principles of their activity in the public sphere. (Johnson 7: 321–332)

Stevenson's "Moral Principle" speech was one of his best and it seems an injustice not to reprint here it in its entirety. Even so, these half dozen selections are illustrative of Stevenson's attention to literary craft.

Stevenson's eloquence with pen and voice as reflected in such speeches was widely recognized. Writing for the *St. Louis Post Dispatch* after Stevenson's second Presidential defeat, journalist Irving Dilliard summed it this way; "Here was a man who brought to politics fresh ideas, moving eloquence, boldness of spirit, and breadth of vision. Intellectually, he was the best prepared candidate since Wilson" (6: 459). His way of saying something was as important as what he said. Carl Sandburg called Stevenson "a moving and eloquent spokesman for the hopes and dreams of the American people" (Sandburg, October 25, 1952). Further, Sandburg recorded in the same speech:

I like it that my friend, John Steinbeck...comes out for Stevenson, saying, "As a writer I love the clear, clean writing of Stevenson. As a man I like the intelligent, humorous, logical, civilized mind." It is more than a compliment, it is an award when a man of Steinbeck's curiosity and insight says another man has an intelligent, humorous, logical, and civilized mind. (October 25, 1952)

Eric Sevareid, one of the most literate and articulate journalists of the twentieth century, said Stevenson

> injected humor and happiness and sophistication into American political life, and you have to have spent half your life listening to the normal run of American politicians to really understand what a fantastic accomplishment that was. (Johnson 1: xvi)

The key *word* from Sevareid's account is "sophistication" since it accentuates the writers' judgment of Stevenson's speaking and writing style as being unusually articulate and eloquent. The key *concept* is that Stevenson's sophistication (articulations, eloquence, urbanity) was not found in the normal run of American politicians.

Among other writers who recognized Stevenson's stylistic uniqueness were the novelist John Hersey, who chaired the Volunteers for Stevenson in Connecticut, and Robert Sherwood, the playwright, who wrote to Stevenson after the 1952 nominating convention describing Stevenson's acceptance speech as "a very great document, intellectually and artistically, as well as politically" (Sherwood, July 26, 1952). And later, in 1958, John Steinbeck would write to William Blair, a mutual friend, "Mr. Stevenson is one of the best writers in the country" (Steinbeck, June 22, 1958). Writers respected the thoughtfulness, energy, and time that Stevenson put into his writing, even if his political advisors did not. George Ball remembered: "We used to tell him that he would rather write than be President" (Fairlie 30). That Stevenson, in fact, may have agreed, appealed to intellectuals.

In reflecting on nearly five decades of covering the political culture of the United States, Godfrey Sperling of the *Christian Science Monitor*, wrote: "I was very impressed with Adlai Stevenson – although he was not an overly friendly fellow. He was by far and away the best speaker I ever covered" (Sperling 19). Stevenson chose to wind his way down the national political road armed with "the shield of reason in one hand, the bow of language in the other, and a quiver full of gags and puns and aphorisms slung across his back" (Morgan 53). Intellectuals adored this posture. They appreciated the articulations and the frequently accompanying levity in Stevenson as much as they enjoyed it in themselves. For them he was truly *le homme d'esprit* among politicos.

William Adler, chronicler of candidate witticisms, has provided ample evidence of Adlai Stevenson's wit (*The Wit and Wisdom of Adlai Stevenson,* 1966), but samples abound wherever Stevenson is the subject. Walter Johnson recounts the following episode in which Stevenson met tragedy with his abiding sense of humor.

> One evening in January, 1938, their home on St. Mary's Road near Libertyville caught on fire. A dispute between local fire companies as to which had jurisdiction and confusion between the crews when they did arrive ended any hope of saving the new home. By the time Adlai and Ellen Stevenson had driven forty miles from Chicago, flames were bursting through the windows and the roof. As a neighbor expressed his sympathy to Stevenson, some burning debris floated through the air and landed at Adlai's feet. He picked it up, lit a cigarette, and said, "Oh well, as you can see, we are still using the house." (Johnson 1: 382)

The heat of the presidential campaigns in 1952 and 1956 seemed to arouse the best of Stevenson's wit. Bill Adler cites the following quips.

> If I talk over the people's heads, Ike must be talking under their feet. (Adler 2)
> I have been much interested in the continued debate raging in the news-papers as to whether I am headed left, center, or right. I think it would be more relevant to ask: Is the man moving forward or backward or is he grounded? (17)
> I have been tempted to make a proposal to our Republican friends: that if they stop telling lies about us, we would stop telling the truth about them. (29)
> Eggheads unite...you have nothing to lose but your yolks. (89)
> Golf is fine release from the tensions of office, but we are a little tired of holding the bag. (29)

This often-told anecdote fuses several themes in this book, including his wit. As Stevenson was delivering a campus speech, a student shouted, "Every thinking man will vote for Governor Stevenson." Stevenson replied, "Thank you very much but I prefer to have the majority vote for me!"

The serious side of Stevenson's eloquence was most likely even of greater appeal to intellectuals. His vast capacity for wit was only one more ingredient for them to appreciate. The content of Stevenson's eloquent and gracious speeches, particularly his attention to internationalist-universalist concerns and his ubiquitous call for reason, was also appealing. In the "Moral Principle" speech, he uttered that greatness is equated with speaking "for humanity at large" and concern for "the whole of man." His was a voice opposed to the worst aspects of provincialism and nationalism. He recognized as famed architect Louis Sullivan had decades before, that to radiate the living qualities of imagination and reflection, one's works must show that one is a "well-wisher to humanity at large, not a stranger to it, and heedless of it" (Sullivan 150).

Throughout his public life, especially since his days at the Chicago Council on Foreign Relations, Stevenson spoke passionately and urgently for a cooperative United States role in "humanity at large." In 1945, more than a half dozen years before he was widely discussed as a possible presidential candidate, he lamented in a London speech that because man's mastery of himself had not kept pace with man's mastery of science, the United States was committed to getting "the UN organized and functioning as quickly as possible" and warned that "it will take the faith, confidence, and energy of all of us to make it work," and that it was "the only practicable alternative" (Johnson 2: 278–80). The formal establishment of the United Nations, and his own role in that process, were satisfying to Stevenson, and he relentlessly hammered at the need to make it work. To the International Astronomical Association, he said: "If there can be said to be a wave of the future for mankind, I believe it is in the principle of community" in which nations "join their sovereign wills" (Stevenson, "Looking Outward" 157). In 1960 he encouraged the newly elected John Kennedy not to be "content to project beyond our frontiers with little but rockets and the threat of destruction. We need to replace our human neighborhood of common work and cooperation" (Johnson 7: 608). This consistent, Wilsonian theme was poignantly expressed in Stevenson's last formal speech in which he pleaded for interdependence. "We travel together, passengers on a little space ship...preserved from annihilation by the care, the work, and the love we give our fragile craft," said Stevenson. "We cannot maintain it," he concluded, "half fortunate, half miserable, half confident, half despairing, half slave...half free.... No craft, no crew can travel safely with such vast contradictions. On their resolution depends the survival of us all" (8: 814–815).

His own moral sensitivity, publicly displayed, also played well in intellectual circles. In the midst of post-war prosperity (1954) Stevenson said, "There is a great hunger among the people for moral leadership...We have placed too much emphasis on materialism. Most political appeals have been to the belly rather than to the spiritual, the intellectual, the moral, and the educational" (Johnson 4: 265). Later, in the same decade, he was still as persistently annoyed with a society that he perceived as having little moral integrity. In a December, 1959 speech, Stevenson harangued:

> There is no real clash of ideas; no new ideas at all...One pitiful cheater on a commercial TV program receives a hundred times the attention paid to four or five million unemployed workers. We don't shake our fists or flex our muscles about anything [important]". (Martin, *World* 465)

This 1959 address echoed earlier speeches. Recall the Godkin lecture in which Stevenson reminded listeners that the foremost contribution to human society by the United States had come "from her ideas; from the moral sentiments of human liberty and human welfare" (112). On a different occasion he said that freedom is neither an ideal nor a protection "if it means nothing more than the freedom to stagnate, to live without dreams, to have no greater aim than a second car and another television set...and this in a world where half our fellow men have less than enough to eat" (Muller 222).

Writers both in the United States and abroad shared his dissatisfaction. American political journalist Richard Rovere: "Stevenson seems a symbol...of political decency and of moral and intellectual integrity" (Graff 34). Historian Henry Steele Commager: "[Stevenson] exercised immense authority wholly without power whose sanctions were entirely intellectual and moral" (Johnson 3: x). *The Times of London*: "[Stevenson] reminded the world that there was another America ... sensitive, self-critical, thoughtful, and visionary. At home he kept the light of intellect burning through a period when it was not fashionable to think" (ix). Indeed, along with his eloquent call for idealism and vision, his faith in the best in human nature and his encouragement to participate in the international community, was a driving desire to make fashionable "to think," to reason.

Stevenson's friend Barbara Ward recalled that he was representative of eighteenth-century Western thinking inasmuch as he possessed "the Enlightenment's cool, Deist religion, its belief in reason and the possibility of progress, its fundamental optimism, and intellectual curiosity" and the belief in "natural law and the community of mankind" (Ward 216). At the United Nations' memorial service for Stevenson, Venezuelan Ambassador Dr. Carlos Sosa Rodriguez referred to him as one of the United Nations' "most enlightened sons" and said that one of Stevenson's greatest attributes was that he was "always convinced of the force of reason" (Johnson 8: viii).

Stevenson himself, perhaps naively, believed that even votes could be secured through reason. "People are educable on the issues; you can, I believe," said Stevenson in a 1956 interview, "induce convictions by reason" (6: ix). Even if he merely were trying to convince himself that reason, in the end, could save humanity, intellectuals rushed to the cause, recognizing that Stevenson's call to reason as campaign fare represented a standard by which they could measure their own political activity. In fact, though he would lose twice to a likely unbeatable Eisenhower, "Stevenson's eloquence and intelligence inspired a generation" (Klinkner 1).

In his classic study of the American voter (1960), social psychologist Angus Campbell found that persons who perceive issues to be more relevant to their values will be more likely to express intense opinions (Campbell 113). Intellectuals perceived that Adlai Stevenson embodied their vision of the world; a world in which language is revered, international good will is promoted and reason prevails. They also believed that apart from Stevenson, most other politicians did not share their vision.

What about Stevenson's style as contrasted with that of other politicians on the national scene in the 1950s? "After all, Washington is a company city: its business, politics; its leaders and aspiring juniors are largely ignorant of literature, history, philosophy and all other realms of thought and discourse not related to the most mundane and practical concerns" (Goodwin 33).

The thought of someone heading the national government who was well- versed in history, literature, and philosophy—in short, someone who was culturally literate and proud to be so was extremely appealing to intellectuals. Consider some of those to whom Stevenson stood in contrast and the point is made clearer. Dwight Eisenhower and Richard Nixon, although politically astute, were not perceived by intellectuals as being particularly literate in the classical sense. Even John F. Kennedy, who would later win the favor of intellectuals, was a distant second when their litmus tests were applied.

I begin with the contrast of Stevenson to Eisenhower, twice his electoral nemesis. As most of the intellectuals of the day saw it, Eisenhower was content with a nation in which, according to William Faulkner, "The artist has no more actual place in the American culture of today than he has in the American economy of today, no place at all in the warp and woof, the thews and sinews, the mosaic of the American dream" (Muller 268). The following quotation from Eric Sevareid provides in greater detail the intellectuals' assessment of the differences between two Presidential candidates in 1952.

> What, after all, is the Eisenhower appeal to people? … He is not only appealing to people's prejudices and animosities and ignorance…more than that, he is appealing to their weary perplexity. Millions of people seem to be tired of trying to think out answers to problems like Russia, Korea, and inflation, that seem to have no clear answers…. [Eisenhower] is saying just trust me and my friends…. He is careful not to ask them to think…. [Stevenson] takes the opposite approach. In his almost painful honesty, he makes clear that he does not know all the answers…and he demands that the people think…. He has been analyzing, not asserting; he has been projecting, not any image of the big, competent father or brother, but of the moral and intellectual proctor.

Sevareid concluded his statement with these telling lines:

> [Stevenson] has revealed…a luminosity of intelligence unmatched on the political scene today; he has caught the imagination of the intellectuals, of all those who are really informed; he has excited the passions of the mind…[Eisenhower], God knows, is empty of ideas or certitude himself. (Johnson 4: 133–134)

While intellectuals could readily accept Stevenson's Niebuhrian (theologian, ethicist, and commentator Reinhold Niebuhr) view that there is a great complexity to life and therefore truly solving most problems is exceedingly difficult, they were apparently appalled that Eisenhower's quicker, simpler, "black and white" rhetoric would play so well among voters. As historian Paul Allen Carter has pointed out so ably, Stevenson was not exempt from Cold War rhetoric, using words such as "dupes" and phrases such as "no place is safe" in campaign speeches (Carter 13), even saying the Red Chinese seem unable to get along with anybody in the world and should, therefore, not be admitted to the United Nations (Severin 148). The difference was that Eisenhower's "trust me," "I shall go to Korea," "That guy [Stevenson] is a smart aleck," "The French have gone astray since they are fifty percent agnostic or atheistic" (Johnson 4: 4, 10) way of approaching problems offended the sensibilities of most intellectuals. They much preferred this from Stevenson: "We want no shackles of the mind or the spirit, no rigid patterns of thought, no iron conformity" (4: 12).

Intellectuals would say that Eisenhower's specialized training at West Point, with its limited exposure to the humanities, was found dramatically lacking when contrasted with Stevenson's Princeton philosophic, idealistic, classic education, emphasizing the humanities (Davis 283). They would also defend their man's indulgence in ironical wit, saying that he used it because he respected the intelligence of the electorate, not because he was a "smart aleck" (Davis 286). "In the end," Irving Howe has written, "they could imagine that Stevenson was just like them…He was not a mere politician but a statesman, a man of culture and learning who reluctantly assumed the burdens of leadership, a well-bred-old-style intellectual with courtly manners and genteel restraint" (Pells 395).

Another view is that Stevenson was not at all "just like them," but that he was at least not the archenemy of intellectuals that Eisenhower was. Two months before the election of 1952, Malcolm Cowley wrote to Kenneth Burke:

Our troubles [protection of intellectuals from the witch-hunts] are an issue in the present election…I doubt that Stevenson can do much for us, but so far, he's fighting on our side and Eisenhower chose a vice-presidential candidate for the sole purpose of working against us. (Jay 307)

And after the election the poet Robert Lowell wrote to his mentor Allen Tate that "Ike is a sort of symbol to me of America' s unintelligent side…all fitness, muscles, smiles, and banality. And Stevenson was terribly better than one had a right to expect. We, too, feel too hurt too laugh" (Hamilton 197). The same month Lowell wrote to friend and poet Peter Taylor that he was "amazed by" Stevenson's eloquence, adding that "you really learn from him" (206).

These kinds of comments from Cowley and Lowell reflect some suspicion about intellectuals' initial willingness to claim Stevenson fully as "one of their own." Cowley's admission of doubt that "Stevenson can do much for us," and Lowell's surprise that Stevenson could be so attractive, notwithstanding, it remains clear that when contrasted with Eisenhower, intellectuals, at the very least, were willing to adopt him.

In *The Political Life of Children* (1986), the child psychiatrist Robert Coles recounts a telling moment during one of his visits to Children's Hospital in Boston in 1956. One of the children noticed that Coles was not wearing the Stevenson button he had worn in an earlier visit. The child offered that "a lot of Stevenson supporters are stuck up! They're college professors." Continuing, the child said: "Eisenhower beat the Nazis. He's strong and he's been a great president. He doesn't talk fancy, he just leads. My father says college people like Stevenson because he's a big talker" (Coles 5). To many voters the choice was just that simple. As columnist George Will wrote in a 2000 editorial: "Stevenson was the darling of the intelligentsia because he lost to the darling of the electorate, Dwight Eisenhower" (Will 7).

Stevenson and recently elected President Eisenhower outside the White House, February 7, 1953

Perhaps an even starker contrast among Stevenson's political contemporaries was Richard M. Nixon. In Lowell's letter to Taylor cited above, he reacts to Nixon's "Checkers" address asking, "Wasn't Nixon's speech the most servile mush you ever heard?" (206). Intellectuals abhorred Nixon's attacks directed at them during the witch-hunts and they equally abhorred his attacks on the one man with whom they identified on the national political landscape. Long after the heated rhetoric of presidential campaigns had cooled, Nixon was still expressing disdain for Stevenson. In his memoirs he recalled that his attitude toward him was "instinctively negative," adding that he felt Stevenson to be "far more veneer than substance...beneath his glibness and mocking wit he was shallow, flippant, and indecisive" (Brodie 307). The feeling was mutual. About Nixon in 1956, Stevenson shared: "He is, I think, the only human being I have ever truly hated" (Cooke 134). However, just before Nixon became President in 1968, a *Life* magazine interviewer asked if he would be an Eisenhower-like president. Interestingly, this was Nixon's response: "I've more of a philosophical bent. I suppose, in a way I'm probably much closer to the kind of politician that Adlai Stevenson was" (307).

In many respects Nixon relished the role of intellectual and was prepared for it. Presidential scholar James David Barber pointed out in *The Presidential Character* (1985) that Richard Nixon was studious, read voraciously, was second in his class at Whittier College, was third in his class at Duke University Law School (Barber 409), and that acquaintances of his youth recall Nixon as an intellectual who was "too intelligent to be much fun" (402). Was his hatred of intellectuals and Stevenson born of jealousy? Did he feel betrayed by the very group who should have been his admirers? Quite possibly. Late in his political career Nixon lamented:

I wish I had more time to read and write. I'm known as an activist and an organizer, but some people have said I'm sort of an egghead in the Republican Party. I don't write as well as Stevenson, but I work at it...I'd like to write two or three books a year, go to one of the fine schools...Oxford for instance...just teach, read, and write. (358)

Read and write Nixon eventually did. His public career abbreviated by Watergate and his subsequent resignation, Nixon used his time to move beyond perfunctory memoirs to write prodigiously about history and politics. Ironically, being kept at arm's length from party affairs until the last few years afforded him additional privacy to live as statesman, and at long last, as scholar. The sheer number of books, none of them short, and none of them trite in subject, perhaps has carved for him a niche in intellectual circles at last. Richard Nixon's earlier lamentations and his subsequent return to prominence as a "writer" considered, it is still true that in the two decades after World War II Stevenson was intellectually acclaimed, Nixon mocked.

Mary McCarthy's attitude was common among American literary intellectuals. In 1952 she wrote to her friend Hannah Arendt that Stevenson was "the only political figure to awaken my curiosity in years," adding that the "Nixon thing is appalling. On a lower level he reminds me of my character Mulcahy [Professor Henry Mulcahy, the villain in McCarthy's *The Groves of Academe* (1952)] in a cheap mass production – there's sort of a groveling sense of justification and threatening inferiority.... The Nixon success, if it's really serious, is too horribly Orwellian to contemplate" (Brightman 8–9). In contrast, McCarthy and others saw in Stevenson "political chic, that figured for his admirers as a discovery, like an art-object" (9). Not surprisingly, Nixon was Stevenson's villain too. He urged the country to be leery of what he called "Nixonland... a place of slander and scare; the land of sly innuendo, the poison pen, the anonymous phone call and hustling, pushing, shoving; the land of smash and grab and anything to win" (Baker 378).

What about John F. Kennedy, Stevenson, and the intellectuals? By 1960 Stevenson was so endeared to intellectuals that virtually all other politicians, including Kennedy, were lumped together as not to be trusted. Arthur Schlesinger has pointed out that Kennedy's intellectual friends, particularly the literary ones, were, in fact, post-inaugural acquaintances (Schlesinger, *Kennedy* 850), and the title of his campaign-yearbook "Kennedy or Nixon: Does It Make Any Difference?" signals significant pre-election suspicions. Eric Sevareid's answer to Schlesinger's questions was "no," it did not make any difference. His contemporary analysis of Nixon and Kennedy was that they were both "junior executive types...the first completely packaged products of the managerial revolution...incapable of great dreams or any true compassion or of a deep emotional commitment to anything but self-advancement" (Davis 492). Historian John

Bartlow Martin saw it the same way, observing that "Kennedy was a politician to his fingertips, and in many ways a rather conventional one." When contrasted directly with Stevenson, Martin perceived Kennedy as "spurious" and "calculating" while Stevenson "displayed an urbanity which appeared genuine" (Martin, *Illinois* 763). Political writer John Steele also recognized the contrast: "The men of John F. Kennedy...talked in cryptic, often barely understandable phrases; Stevenson talked in long sentences, comma-struck with parenthetical, often qualifying phrases. He was epigrammatic, enjoyed discourse for discourse's sake" (Steele 3). Norman Cousins, publisher of the *Saturday Review*, shared the suspicion and the discouragement. After he was asked by Kennedy partisans to join "the writing team," Cousins wrote to Stevenson that his heart was not in it and added: "Oh, I'll vote for him all right; but it would help if I could think of a good reason for becoming enthusiastic. What I mean is, does Kennedy have any stature?" (Martin, *World* 536). Hannah Arendt wrote to Mary McCarthy: "It looks like Kennedy or Nixon. It is rather nauseating" (Brightman 82).

As President, however, Kennedy carefully cultivated his relationship with intellectuals and once quipped that he had read more books in a week than Stevenson had in a year (Baker 399). He won over many of them and incited many to political action with his call for critical thinking and interest in culture. He appointed at least a dozen Rhodes Scholars and eighteen percent of his appointments were university or foundation people (six percent of Eisenhower's appointments were from universities or foundations, forty-two percent from business) (Barber 315). An optimistic Malcolm Cowley wrote to Kenneth Burke in February of 1961: "We can visit Washington without feeling, as I have for the past twelve years, that I was skulking into enemy territory disguised as a businessman" (Jay 338). Hannah Arendt, her earlier doubts subsiding, praised Kennedy for having "emptied the Harvard faculty" into his administration (Apple 2). The Kennedys became well noted for their White House galas, at which representatives from cultural interests were guests of honor, although the president was reported to have cracked jokes behind his wife's back about the *soirees* she arranged (2).

Even Stevenson, ever armed with historical and literary allusions, saw the growing shift of an old allegiance. In losing the spotlight to Kennedy at the 1960 Democratic National Convention in Los Angeles he said, "Do

Stevenson and Democratic Party nominee John Kennedy on the porch of Kennedy's Hyannis Port, Massachusetts home, on July 31, 1960

you remember in classical times when Cicero finished speaking, the people said, 'How well he spoke,' but when Demosthenes had finished speaking, they said 'Let us march!'" (Brodie 421). But critic Alfred Kazin wrote that "In 1956 even more than in 1952, and at Los Angeles in 1960 even more than in 1956 he [Stevenson] seemed the peerless leader of intellectuals who boasted that they had never had a candidate before…they could never be that much concerned again; they would have suffered just too much" (Solotaroff 234).

Yet, it was Stevenson who consistently stood in contrast to the field, and it is he who is most frequently described as the exception to the rule of intellectual mediocrity in American Presidential politics. Intellectuals judged him as a politician with integrity, who was intelligent, eloquent, and devoted to thought; "a rare bird among politicians" (Walton 227).

Something else drew intellectuals to Stevenson, something they found in him that they felt within themselves. In his investigation into the mixture of politics and culture, Irving Howe found evidence which seemed to indicate that Stevenson's appeal to intellectuals may have developed because he so vividly symbolized their own mixed feelings toward politics itself (Howe, *Steady Work* 207).

Those mixed feelings to which Howe referred are probably the near total indifference to the mundane affairs of politics on the one hand, and the potential for human progress to be shown by certain political achievements on the other. That is, intellectuals will at times be forced to admit that the very political activity toward which they have such aversion may result in a better quality of life for a significant number of people. Their collective political action, in other words, may combat an intellectual life that might be considered merely a case of sentimental, private frivolity.

Here, too, there are shreds of a satisfactory explanation regarding the link between Stevenson and the intellectuals. As I pointed out earlier, Stevenson had his own clear understanding of the nature of American society and what values ought to prevail in that society. His strict adherence to principles so often made him appear to be committing political suicide. Someone once told him that "if you keep doing that [adhering strictly to principles] you can't win." Stevenson replied: "I don't *have* to win" (Fairlie 28). His own mixed feelings about seeking power and securing it may have baffled his political advisors, but it very well could have been a point of endearment to intellectuals.

Eugene McCarthy, himself an intellectual in politics, was able to capture this sensibility when he nominated Stevenson for President in 1960. He addressed the Democratic National Convention in Los Angeles:

He did seek power for himself in 1952. He did not seek power in 1956.... He does not seek it for himself today....This man knows, as all of us do from history, that power often comes to those who seek it. But history does not prove that power is always well used by those who seek it. (McCarthy 211)

This reluctance to seek power, this hesitation, this indecision was quite often accompanied by humor and ridicule. An Illinois political boss related that Stevenson regarded politics with "wholesome apathy" (White 66). And a frequently heard anecdote referring to Stevenson's attitude had him saying, "Do I have time to go to the bathroom?" Followed by: "Do I want to go to the bathroom?" (Halberstam 23). He did seem a reluctant candidate. Even during the campaign for Governor of Illinois in 1948, he already was expressing misgivings about the acquisition of political clout.

He wrote to long-time friend Alicia Patterson: "and why the hell do I want to win and get into that hideous mess for four years of solitary agony and heartbreak?" (Johnson 2: 543). In a letter to Charles Murphy, coun-selor to President Truman, he indicated that he did "not want to run for President.... That I am, aside from the President, the best available man to assume this monstrous task, seems grotesque" (Baker 56). Stevenson's words are an echo to his grandfather's view when he was asked by Grover Cleveland to join the ticket in 1892 as the Democratic candidate for Vice-President. The elder Stevenson said, that saying "yes" was "a dreadful, self-inflicted penance for the good of the country" (130).

Not all Stevenson acquaintances perpetuated the perception of hesita-tion and indecision. Many close to Stevenson believed, in Richard Norton Smith's words, that he had both "a silver tongue and sharp elbows" (Smith 15). Illinois Democratic Party boss Jacob Arvey would write after Stevenson's death: "I am greatly amused at the stories that Adlai Stevenson was indecisive. He was not a superficial man. He insisted upon knowing everything about his subjects. He did not do anything impulsively...but wanted to know every facet of a problem before he decided upon action" (Arvey 54). Stevenson's friend Carl McGowen shared Arvey's view.

> The idea that he was a fish out of water among politicians is a myth. He did wear Brooks Brothers suits. He did wear button down collars. He did have friends in the upper social levels. But he did like politicians, and they liked him, and he had a strong sense of party loyalty. He and Mayor Daley were always close friends...he handled the legislators, the farmers, the small-town lawyers remarkably well. They never talked about his Brooks Brothers suits or called him a Hamlet. In fact, some of them thought he was a little too decisive. (McKeever 158)

Despite Arvey's and McGowen's recollections, the perception persisted. Intellectuals seemed to appreciate Stevenson's aloofness and hesitation more than other groups. Moreover, they were "flattered to see Stevenson in their own plumage: urbane, courteous, able to turn a phrase (even if it said nothing), with a patrician languor that lent the above-the-battle appearance of sacrifice, even of martyrdom for the public good" (Fairlie 27).

To see their own attitudes acted out upon the public stage was appar-ently a pleasing and appealing experience for intellectuals, though not for Stevenson's purely political friends and foes. During the Presidential cam-paign of 1960, Robert Kennedy, who was directing his brother's nomina-tion drive, expressed bitterness toward both Stevenson and the intellectuals who continued to support his candidacy. A frustrated Kennedy quipped:

> Action or success makes them [the intellectuals] suspicious and they almost lose interest. I think that is why so many of them think Adlai Stevenson is

the second coming. But he never quite arrives there; he never quite accomplishes anything…. They like it much better to have a cause than to have a course of action that's been successful. (Schlesinger, *Kennedy* 387)

The attraction in Stevenson's reluctance, hesitation, and aloofness well may be captured by the "common plumage" concept expressed by Fairlie. But perhaps a more reasonable assessment of the relationship is that Stevenson reflected the same complexity of life with which so many intellectuals wrestled in their own work. For them, to see someone on the national political scene share their ambivalence, that "gray area" in life, was not something to be feared; rather, it was a sign of maturity and wisdom. In a 1989 article for *The Atlantic*, Glenn Tinder touched on this very idea when he wrote that hesitation:

expresses a consciousness of the mystery of being and the dignity of every person. It provides a moment for consulting destiny…. It is a formality that is fitting when we cross the frontier between meditation and action…. And like all formalities it is a mark of respect. (Tinder 85)

Is recognizing that intellectuals and Stevenson crossed "the frontier" between thought and action together enough to explain this unusual endearment? I think not. That the intellectuals' ambivalence about the nature of politics seemed to coincide with Stevenson's is more compelling. Significantly, they did not just see him as the best of the available alternatives. In adoring the complexity that mirrored their own, they came to love the composite Stevenson. American writer Dawn Powell, author of sixteen novels and ten plays, although never fully committed to politics, was "delighted by the easy humor and patrician intelligence of Adlai Stevenson…joined a group of "Volunteers for Stevenson"…and was disgusted by the current crop of Republicans who acted as if America has no future and no hope" (Page 255).

To intellectuals, Adlai Stevenson was unique among professional politicians. His qualified liberalism, his academic, cultural, and intellectual heritage, his eloquence and wit, his internationalist views, his call for reason, his idealistic and spiritual nature, his distinction when contrasted with political contemporaries, his own mixed feelings about political power; all of these, to some degree or another, are reasonable explanations for the gathering of "savants and artists" around him. I believe, however, that the list, though lengthy, is incomplete. Scant organized attention has been given elsewhere to the possibility that Stevenson's endearment to intellectuals was based, to a significant degree, on his appeal to them as equals, as peers in the pursuit of a culturally literate nation. The following chapter is devoted to that possibility.

Adlai Stevenson the reader and the writer

The Terms of Endearment

Abstract Chapter 4 brings to the forefront the central reason for the intensity of the relationship: the co-equal manner in which Stevenson treated literary intellectuals: mutually admiring and respectful.

Keywords Correspondence • Flattery • Equality • Sophistication • Advocacy

> *You know, when you have relations, as a writer with public men, there has to be equality…it's an ideal to be aspired to by both writers and public persons.*
> —Robert Lowell (Mazzaro 64)

The list of literary and academic intellectuals who supported Adlai Stevenson seems inexhaustible. Add to that group professionals in the writing "business" … publishers, editors, syndicated columnists, and the number swells. Some, such as Archibald MacLeish and John Steinbeck, were well known to the general public. Others were less well known outside cultural circles at the time. Journalists, critics, and novelists Marya Mannes, Harold "Doc" Humes from New York and Thomas Bryce Morgan from Illinois were among the latter. The more familiar "business" names were columnists Mary McGrory, Doris Fleeson, Marquis Childs,

C. B. Bultman, *Adlai E. Stevenson and American Intellectuals*, https://doi.org/10.1007/978-3-031-80648-3_4

Ralph McGill, editor of the *Atlanta Constitution*, Walter Jones, editor of the *Sacramento Bee*, James Wechsler, Herbert Agar, and Martha (Gellhorn) Matthews, and publishers Agnes Meyer (the *Washington Post*), Dorothy Schiff (*The New York Post*), and Barry Bingham (the *Louisville Courier-Journal*). Many university presidents, such as Robert Hutchins at the University of Chicago and David Owen at Bradley University, were early and steadfast Stevenson supporters.

These kinds of relationships, in many cases, began well before Stevenson's candidacies for President. His attachment to MacLeish, which is reviewed in Chap. 4, originated during World War II. Many literary artists and academics opened their lines of communication and friendship during Stevenson's years as Governor of Illinois (1949–1952) and were frequent visitors at the mansion in Springfield. Interestingly, as Stevenson began his tenure as governor, Ellen Borden Stevenson (Mrs. Adlai Stevenson) became president of the Modern Poetry Association, publisher of *Poetry Magazine*. Knowing that Stevenson's marriage to Ellen did not survive the year, it is incidental and unlikely that her involvement in the arts had much at all to do with her husband's life-long endearment to intellectuals. It was Adlai Stevenson himself they loved.

Evidence abounds that Stevenson's enduring friendships with intellectuals were based on the acknowledgement that they were equals. He was stirred by mutual involvement with writers during his entire lifetime; the Stevenson family's intimacy with Illinois poet Vachel Lindsay provides an early example. In October of 1914, Stevenson's father Lewis Green Stevenson was appointed to fill the unexpired term of the Secretary of State of Illinois, who had committed suicide earlier that month. Moving from Bloomington to the capital fostered an enlarged cultural circle for Adlai, then just fourteen years old. On the many occasions when Lindsay was a dinner guest at the Stevenson home, he was asked to read his poetry. Family members recalled Stevenson being "stirred by" selections such as "Eagle Forgotten," "Bryan, Bryan, Bryan," and "Abraham Lincoln Walks at Midnight" (Johnson 3: 132). Stevenson's sister Elizabeth later recalled: "I realize now how much Adlai was absorbing...from poets as well as politicians" (Ives, *My Brother* 80).

Years later, when the Lindsay family residence, which was adjacent to the governor's mansion, had fallen into great disrepair, then Governor Stevenson used his public influence to review a faltering and ineffective Vachel Lindsay Association to promote restoration of the homestead. "The Lindsay House was saved for ages to be when Adlai took the idea enthusiastically," wrote one Stevenson friend to another (Johnson 3: 132).

Lindsay's sister Olive Lindsay Wakefield, herself an aspiring writer, later gave Stevenson an assortment of her brother's papers, including letters and poems. He, in turn, spoke favorably about her various writing projects and encouraged her to finish two books on which she was working (200). He cared for writers, even the less well known, and they cared for him. Respect, admiration, and equality were mutual attitudes.

A very special guest at the governor's mansion was another Illinois poet, Carl Sandburg. Sandburg spoke at Stevenson's inauguration in January of 1949 and stayed at the mansion the first night Stevenson occupied it (Davis 198). Sandburg rarely accepted such speaking invitations; "I turn down ten for every one I accept," he said (Mitgang, *Letters* 456). Though they had known each other before, from that time on the Stevenson-Sandburg relationship grew. Their correspondence to and about each other indicates a rapport born of equality. Stevenson's words are not those of a politician who dismissed intellectual as apart from "the real world." Likewise, Sandburg's words are not those of a poet who dismissed politicians as having no sensibilities save that of the lust for power.

In the spring of 1952, fully three months before Adlai Stevenson would accept the Democratic presidential nomination, Sandburg wrote to Stevenson that he was "carrying around" Stevenson speeches from a recent tour of New York, adding: "Your speech has paragraphs and sentences that I have read several times...profound thinking, subtle feeling, exactitude of phrasing...great utterances for this hour and for many tomorrows" (Johnson 3: 562). Stevenson's response exemplifies more than cordiality. He thanked Sandburg for the letter and continued: "When Sandburg carries around Stevenson speeches, it's news...or perhaps it is sinister evidence of a pitiful deterioration in Sandburg's literary tastes.... Anyway, I am bursting with pride" (562).

Stevenson's sincere gratitude for the accolades of a prominent literary figure and his almost giddy surprise at Sandburg's attention are revealing. The mutual admiration would continue. A week before the 1952 election Sandburg spoke on Stevenson's behalf at a Madison Square Garden rally. "I have known Adlai Stevenson for twenty-five years," he said, "and I am not cutting any corners nor shading any phrase when I say that he is a great and consecrated man, one more embodiment of the finest human flames out of America's past" (Johnson 4: 175). Sandburg shared the grief at the disheartening loss to Eisenhower, writing to Stevenson: "You are cherished and remembered in a multitude of deep prayers" (192).

Communication between the two men persisted. Stevenson took the opportunity in September of 1954 to thank Sandburg for a recent letter:

"These little notes now and then do something to me...something very good. Bless you" (397). In the same letter, Stevenson lamented that he would not be able to attend a reception in Chicago celebrating Sandburg's recent publication of *Abraham Lincoln: The Prairie and War Years* (397). A few months later further evidence of the co-equal flattery was to be found in this short note from Stevenson to Sandburg: "I hear that in Louisville you said that Adlai Stevenson could 'tell you what to do.' Okay, you asked for it... (1) Live forever, and (2) never pass this way without letting me know." The note closed with "Affectionately" (451).

In other letters Sandburg would tell Stevenson that his speeches and ideas were "better than ever, the best since Lincoln" (Johnson 6: 283), and that "You wear well and are kept deep in many hearts" (7: 366). Amid international travels and domestic political forays, Stevenson always responded with humility and reciprocal praise. I think it is noteworthy that the reciprocity with Sandburg (and as I will point out, with other literary intellectuals as well), was not a private matter. In a Columbia Broadcasting System radio spot in 1955 Stevenson made the following remarks about Sandburg:

> Carl Sandburg is one of the few living men whose work and whose life epitomizes the American Dream. He has seen the earthiness of the prairies, the majesty of mountains, the anger of deep inland seas. In him is the restlessness of the seeker, the questioner, the explorer of horizons, the hunger that is never satisfied. In him is also the tough strength that has never been fully measured, never unleashed, the resiliency of youthfulness which no aging can destroy. (Johnson 4: 452)

Perhaps no other occasion reflects this mutuality better than Stevenson's words on Sandburg's eighty-fifth birthday in 1963, "a day on which to celebrate the many blessings that are Carl Sandburg" (Johnson 8: 369). Stevenson described Sandburg as "the poet who has heard the heartland of America singing," "the generous custodian of American folksongs," a "matchless scholar and historian," "seer, sage, philosopher," and "raconteur extraordinary" (369). Stevenson concluded his remarks with an acknowledgment particularly welcome to a writer: "I have unblushingly borrowed phrases from Carl Sandburg since my entry into public speaking" (369).

One could argue that these two connections (Stevenson and Lindsay and Stevenson and Sandburg) were natural, and representative of nothing more than three prominent figures and their families weaving an affinity sparked by the central prairie of Illinois. The reality is otherwise.

Stevenson's link to intellectuals had no geographic boundaries. Neither were there boundaries of genre or literary occupation, as the mutual appeal included poets, novelists, playwrights, essayists, critics, and academics. I return, then, to additional expressions of equality apart from those of Lindsay and Sandburg, but reserve special attention to Stevenson's relationship with Archibald MacLeish and John Steinbeck for succeeding chapters.

One recurring ingredient in Stevenson's deliberate message of equality with intellectuals, and a strikingly ironic one, was his own public and private subordination to them. At the funeral of his Libertyville neighbor and Civil War chronicler, Lloyd Lewis, an event cited earlier, Stevenson was at what some observers felt his eloquent best. Also in attendance as a speaker that day was the playwright Marc Connelly, a founding member of the Algonquin Round Table and perhaps best known for the Pulitzer Prize winning *The Green Pastures* (1930), a biblical fantasy. Recalling the event to Irving Dilliard, Editor of the *St. Louis Post-Dispatch*, Stevenson wrote that "Marc Connelly made a beautiful talk, and I followed with a few choked and incoherent remarks" (Johnson 3: 78). And to Edwin Lahey of the *Chicago Daily News*, he described Marc Connelly as "the speaker" and himself as "a poor second" (80). Six years later Stevenson expressed disappointment that he had missed a Connelly visit to Illinois "because I have wanted to ask you a long while if your wonderful "O! Caesar" story has ever been printed…a copy of which I could read again and again" (Johnson 4: 549). Stevenson's interest in Connelly's literary success matches perfectly Connelly's support for Stevenson's political quests.

The correspondence between Stevenson and another playwright, Robert Sherwood, who won the Pulitzer Prize for *Idiot's Delight* in 1936, amplifies the equality theme. The spring of 1952 was an anxious time for Adlai Stevenson. The decision to run for President not yet made, he was under tremendous pressure from many circles, including intellectuals, to become a candidate. Sherwood was one of many who saw Stevenson as the Democrats' strongest choice and urged him to run. In response to Sherwood's urging, Stevenson wrote about the mounting pressure he was under but ended with, "You have flattered me profoundly by writing me and I shall value your letter always" and in a post-script invited Sherwood to visit him in Libertyville (Johnson 3: 558).

Once Stevenson was nominated, the mutual admiration intensified. A delighted Sherwood wrote Stevenson about the "supreme appropriateness" of the nomination, thanked Stevenson for "the nobility and courage and good humor" with which he accepted it, and told him that the acceptance speech was "a very great document, intellectually, artistically, as well as politically," giving it "the highest praise" that he "could give any speech" (Johnson 4: 21). In typical fashion, Stevenson's reply encouraged closer ties to Sherwood, saying that the letter had touched him deeply. Then, amazingly, amid a full-blown race for the Presidency, Stevenson again invited Sherwood to Illinois, even going so far as to advise Sherwood of the travel times from Chicago to Springfield by train and plane, and offered to send a car to pick him up "if that is more convenient" (22). They would meet as old friends in England the following summer (Johnson 5: 400).

Two years later (1955), Stevenson took time from his usual busy schedule to drop a hospitalized Sherwood a get-well note. A recovering Sherwood sent Stevenson a thank-you letter and enclosed a *Fortune* article he had written. Again, the typical Stevenson retort was full of humility and praise, claiming in this case, "regret" that he had not written the article himself (Johnson 4: 55).

Among the many novelists who were recipients of Stevenson's attitude of equality was James T. Farrell. Most famous for his Studs Lonigan trilogy, Farrell's proletarian upbringing in the south Chicago slums seems the antithesis to Stevenson's protected and privileged heritage. But here, too, the mutual respect was solid. Since the election of 1952, Stevenson's oratorical skills were widely known and Farrell was surely not alone in continuing to follow carefully Stevenson's public utterances. In 1954, and all the way from Paris, Farrell acclaimed a recent speech at Columbia University and requested copies of it. Stevenson obliged Farrell by forwarding the address but, predictably, deflected praise in thanking Farrell for his "most interesting letter" and adding, "My how you can write!" (379). After the election of 1956, Farrell was more than laudatory in a letter to the defeated Stevenson, saying: "What I want to do is to express my great admiration for you, for the campaign you have waged, and for the honesty you brought to American politics" (Johnson 6: 343). Thanking writers for useful phrases, or just acknowledging precision in language was another Stevenson habit that revealed his commitment to equality. In response to Farrell's letter, for example, he was quick to say, "I loved your line about" (343). Or later, in another letter, "I must thank you for a great phrase" (354).

The novelist John Hersey, who headed the Volunteers for Stevenson in Connecticut, received the same kind of Stevenson humility, grace, and appreciation for craft. To Hersey:

I hope very much that I am not presuming upon you. When I learned that your helping me out will interrupt your work on your novel, I couldn't help feeling that this represents a very improper balancing of values. I am afraid that I am becoming calloused to this business of imposing on other people. But please don't let this interfere too much. (167)

Imagine a Presidential candidate, seeking the most powerful position in the world, "interfering" with the intellectual work of a novelist!

Other novelists experienced Stevenson's sincere regard for their work. To Eugene Burdick, author of *The Ugly American* (1958), Stevenson wrote that he liked to keep three copies of the book around to prove to visitors "that he knew the guy"; adding, "And I now can put an autographed copy in the guest room...and what an autograph" (Johnson 7: 301). And to Pearl S. Buck, Pulitzer and Nobel winner and surveyor of Chinese life, he paid this compliment: "Certainly Asia is more important to America than America is to Asia just now, and who can tell us more about it than you" (312).

Even a "one hundred percent old-line Republican" was in the mode of mutual admiration. Taylor Caldwell wrote Stevenson in 1959 with the conclusion that he had been treated unfairly by the print media and that she was forwarding to him a copy of her latest book. Stevenson responded:

I was delighted with your engaging letter. It was good enough for a Democrat. Indeed, it was too good...I shall look forward to "Dear And Glorious Physician," and I am profoundly flattered that you are going to send me an autographed copy. I will do the same for you with a little volume of newspaper pieces that Harper's is putting out in March...in a full and busy life I have missed you too, and that I hope to be able to remedy someday ... and soon, I hope. With my warm regards and admiration. (334)

This letter is particularly instructive since it shows not only the ever-gracious Stevenson, but also shows a politician genuinely interested in the literary work of a writer whom he had never met. Indeed, Stevenson seemed put out by not having met Miss Caldwell and more than eager for the "remedy." Note, too, the line "I will do the same for you." Although Caldwell would be recognized more as a writer of "best sellers" than of "great literary works" better regarded by intellectuals, the tone of the letter is consistent with the others used in this project; in all of them Stevenson established the necessary elements for equality and then expected no less. One cannot help but wonder if Stevenson knew at the time that Caldwell "wrote for the John Birch Society and belonged to the far-Right Liberty League" (Brown 46).

To further validate the importance of the "equality factor" in the Stevenson-intellectual equation, consider the following additional relationships. Vincent Sheehan, author, and foreign correspondent, was a long-time Stevenson supporter who often sent words of encouragement. To Sheehan's praise in the aftermath of securing the nomination in 1952, Stevenson quickly leveled the field with "if only I could write like you my trepidation would subside" and, of course, invited Sheehan to visit him in Illinois (Johnson 4: 33). Nearly eight years later Sheehan, who was still corresponding with Stevenson about political and literary matters, forwarded Stevenson a copy of his latest book, *Nehru: The Years of Power* (1959). In the heart of Stevenson's reply was: "I look forward to your book and am more grateful than I can tell you for the inscription" (Johnson 7: 373). In 1960, Sheehan was among the vast group of intellectuals who desperately wanted Stevenson to run for President again. Apparently, somewhere in his missive, Sheehan adopted the Stevenson characteristic of begging forgiveness for the awkwardly written letter. Not to be outdone, Stevenson told him, "I wish I had such 'clumsy and insufficient' words as you have" (383).

American historian and critic Bernard DeVoto, who worked for the Stevenson campaign in 1952, also heaped flattery on him, calling the campaign "the most honorable, distinguished and truthful campaign in American history." Stevenson, always deflecting the attention, and in doing so creating even more of it among intellectuals, wrote to DeVoto that one of the "blessings" of losing was "the opportunity, at last, to read a little DeVoto and his latest book" (*The Course of Empire* 1952) (Johnson 4: 200). Using a January *Harper's* article in 1955, which claimed that "eggheads are indispensable to the Democratic Party," DeVoto pushed Stevenson especially hard toward the nomination in 1956. In a letter to DeVoto agreeing with that premise, Stevenson added that he was not sure "just how indispensable" he was "to the Party or the eggheads" (442).

Adlai Stevenson's message of equality with intellectuals took many forms. Here, I have focused on letters, notes, and speeches in which he consistently blunted praise by intellectuals while at the same time fueling their own egos. But Stevenson scored points with intellectuals, too, by serving as an advocate for them in a variety of ways. Stevenson, for example, frequently on his own initiative, as well as at the request of intellectuals, introduced them to people of power and prestige who did not travel in their circles. That pattern went back to his days on the Chicago Council of Foreign Relations, and particularly after being elected its president in 1935. He became in the 1930s the Council's conduit to men and women of exceptional learning. The record reveals Stevenson welcoming a great number of journalists and professors as featured speakers before the Council (Johnson 1: 571n).

Thirty years later the importance Stevenson placed on such activity had not changed. When asked by President Kennedy to suggest names for the make-up of the United States delegation to the United Nations, Stevenson recommended several people by emphasizing their talents as writers. One was Jonathan Daniels, whom Stevenson described as a "sophisticated man...has written good books." Daniels was editor of the *Raleigh News and Observer*, author of *Robert E. Lee* (1960) and *Ordeal of Ambition: Jefferson, Hamilton, and Burr* (1970), and had served in Franklin Roosevelt's administration. Another he described as a "well-known writer" with "ideas for your administration" (Johnson 7: 614) was the novelist-journalist John Gunther, who was planning a trip through Latin America the summer that Stevenson died, and requested from Stevenson a letter of introduction to Eduardo Frei Montalva, the President of Chile (Johnson 8: 673).

Stevenson's efforts on behalf of intellectuals went much further than introductions, of course. In 1958, Stevenson went to Moscow "to represent the Author's League in an effort to obtain royalties for books and plays written by its members and translated in the Soviet Union" (Mitgang 246). Stevenson described the endeavor to one of his Chicago law partners Joseph Iseman.

I am strongly under the impression that we touched a deep and sensitive cord [sic] and that they want to do something both to clean up the account and to restore respect among intellectuals as well as to encourage the publication of Soviet books abroad. (Johnson 7: 281)

In Stevenson's own account of the excursion, he noted that among the highest paid Soviet citizens were "the great scholars and scientists" (Stevenson, *Friends* 38n).

The visit was successful for the Author's League and for Stevenson, as his own stature among intellectuals was enhanced.

Stevenson's advocacy of intellectuals was clear. He decried the tendency in the United States "to turn upon our thinkers, to sneer at intellectuals" (Martin, *World* 188), and was willing to align himself with a group hardly able to repay such advocacy with political clout. Sensitive to the work of intellectuals, and to the craft of putting ideas into print in particular, Stevenson felt their burden better than any politician of his age. Because of his own passion for precise and eloquent communication, he understood that creativity is not easy labor. He despaired when because of mundane political obligations he was unable to write and read to his satisfaction.

He also sensed the propensity for despair among intellectuals, whose life's work revolved daily around the cultivation of ideas and reflection about them, while the general public remained essentially unconcerned.

Had he been elected President, Stevenson probably would have found, as Vaclav Havel did in Czechoslovakia, that bridging the purely intellectual world and the practical world of politics an immense task. In 1991, *Newsweek* asked Havel if he had time to write and read since becoming president. He responded: "I am constantly fighting for the time...I have no time to read other things than newspapers, official papers, draft laws. From time to time, I leaf through a book, but is absolutely impossible for me to read fiction" ("Parallels" 31). Likewise, those intellectuals who were drawn into the sphere of political power-brokering through their attachment to Stevenson surely realized the truth in Havel's perception that "it is much easier to sit at home and write about things than to rule" (31).

Havel's answer harks back to the general discussion in Chap. 1 about intellectuals in positions of political power. So does the following observation by Jose Figueres, President of Chile in the 1950s. After Figueres had read Stevenson's book *Call to Greatness* (1954), a collection of his Godkin Lectures, he tapped that recurrent theme in a letter to Arthur Schlesinger, Jr., writing:

> Being still under the emotions of his [Stevenson's] book, I wonder once more where a thinking man is more useful...as president of a republic or behind a typewriter. With all their advantages, modern republics have made Plato's philosopher-king impossible. (Johnson 4: 430)

Impossible? Perhaps, but the perception by intellectuals in Stevenson's day was that it should be tried. In this chapter I have framed the idea that the intellectuals' belief in Stevenson was matched evenly by his belief in them. He treated creative writers and academics as peers, as colleagues, in short, as equals, mutually respected and appreciated. And Stevenson was never embarrassed by such substantial terms of endearment. To long-time intimate Alicia Patterson, he wrote: "I hope it doesn't become subversive in the land of Jefferson to like intelligent, educated, sensitive people or to be proud that they voted for you" (223).

In 1962 Stevenson used the pages of *The New Republic* to articulate not only his personal respect for intellectuals, but society's obligation to them as well. In the article, largely a tribute to the aging Robert Frost, Stevenson recalled that poets often pay tribute to statesmen (Vergil, Dante) and asked what public servants can do for poets. He answered that

public servants are obligated to defend a society which ensures the freedom to create and added that "that is all the poet needs from society; the
rest, the power to reveal truth…he has inside himself" (Stevenson, "Robert
Frost" 27). Here, then, was a politician who lauded intellectuals, in this
example creative writers, as revealers of truth. They in turn lauded him as
one of their own.

One could raise the objection that most of the writers mentioned in this
chapter, including MacLeish and Steinbeck, were "middle-brow," second-
rate figures in American culture. Does such criticism bolster the idea that
Stevenson attracted only the second-rate because he, and they, were both
second-rate? I do not believe so.

The whole notion of rating writers has become increasingly problematic and is compounded by the reluctance of critics to elevate many writers
to the status of "great" in any age. Who were the first-rate writers during
the years of Stevenson's greatest visibility? Faulkner and Hemingway perhaps? Just because neither of them openly supported Stevenson does not
diminish the argument that Stevenson attracted intellectuals, as broadly
defined in this study. Faulkner, incidentally, actually voted for Eisenhower
because to elect Stevenson, whom he thought would be another president
on the Left, would be to guarantee the presidency for Senator Joseph
McCarthy in the next election (Karl 847n). Faulkner did acknowledge,
consistent with the judgment of many others, that Stevenson's "three
strikes were wit, urbanity and erudition" (945). Similarly, Hemingway
could not bring himself to vote for Stevenson, yet he told his wife Mary
that an Eisenhower speech he had heard recently was "the least inspiring
pre-assault sh-- [he] had been unprivileged to listen to" (Baker 862). One
should also not forget that MacLeish, Steinbeck, and others referred to in
this section, while they may have detractors, also have critics who view
them as writers of the first rank.

At any rate, the list of intellectuals, both creative and scholarly, who
joined the clamor below by becoming actively involved in Stevenson's
campaigns is impressive and undeniable. Not only did Stevenson attract
their private, often emotional support, he attracted their public support as
well. They saw in Stevenson a chance to finally have in politics a man
whose vision, introspection and eloquence would lead, as Carl Sandburg
said, with "hope of great days to come, great days possible to men and
women of will and vision" (Johnson 4: 175). Two men whose private and
public support of Stevenson strikes me as particularly representative of the
intensity with which so many of these associations were forged are
Archibald MacLeish and John Steinbeck. Case studies of their relationships to Stevenson follow in Chaps. 4 and 5.

Archibald MacLeish, Librarian of Congress, 1943

Adlai Stevenson and Archibald Macleish

Abstract Chapter 5 is the first of the book's two case studies which accentuate the deeply personal relationship forged by Stevenson and individual members of the literary-intellectual community. The chapter illumines the affinity that Stevenson and MacLeish had for each other, through their mutual understanding and respect.

Keywords Service • Propaganda • Obligations • Humility • Reverence • Honorable • Creative

> *What a remarkable man you are and how proud I am to call*
> *you friend.*
> —Stevenson to MacLeish (Johnson, 7: 350)

> *Adlai, my boy, I salute you! I revere you...I love you!*
> —MacLeish to Stevenson (Johnson 3: 141)

Gerald Murphy, the perennial host to intellectuals at his home in the south of France, once said that "we all loved Adlai Stevenson" (Donnelly xiii). To the extent that this was the case, it was also true that some loved him more than others. The correspondence among intellectuals of the 1950s and 1960s, as well as Stevenson's own correspondence with them, certainly verifies the notion that he was widely admired, respected, and revered, though not by those on the far left, who saw Stevenson as a corruptible man of the middle.

Numerous writers, even those likely to be judged as apolitical, at the very least commented on the Stevenson candidacies in positive ways. Poet Delmore Schwartz, for example, mused in a 1952 letter that perhaps it was time "to choose between literature [Stevenson?] and the G.O.P." (Phillips 265). Novelist Carson McCullers was "disappointed when Adlai Stevenson did not win the nomination in 1960" (Carr 485). Writer Jean Stafford was quite obviously more than disappointed. A recent biography recounts the following post-1952 election episode involving a discussion with her husband, Oliver Jensen. Stafford asked, "Well, now, you tell me. Who did you vote for?" "Eisenhower," Jensen replied. Enraged, Stafford ran upstairs, slammed the door, and called a friend to come and get her "because," said Stafford, "I will never spend another night under the same roof as that man" (Roberts 301). The friend did come, and she disappeared into New York City for several days. The disappointment at Stevenson's defeats in intellectual circles was pervasive, indeed. In a recent biography of Elizabeth Hardwick, writer, and co-founder of *The New York Review of Books*, and second wife of poet Robert Lowell, Hardwick is recalled as saying, "When Eisenhower won in a landslide victory, the Lowells—like other American intellectuals—were devastated" (Curtis 93). And though not yet in full bloom as a noted writer, Smith College sophomore Sylvia Plath responded to Stevenson's 1952 defeat with: "I felt that it was the funeral day of all my hopes and ideas" (Wagner-Martin 90).

But others, like Archibald MacLeish, developed long-term relationships with Stevenson which reflected a deeper affinity than that expressed merely at the ballot box or in private disappointments. A careful look at the MacLeish-Stevenson connection illumines a relationship which was at once political and profoundly personal.

Archibald MacLeish and Adlai Stevenson were contemporaries. Though MacLeish would outlive Stevenson by seventeen years, they were born within six years of each other, and during the lives that followed they witnessed tumultuous times. They experienced the horror of the two world wars, the anxiety and pain of the depression that split those wars, and the ubiquitous ideological battles of the first half of the twentieth century.

They were, however, more than chronological contemporaries; they were soul mates as well. Surely, the spiritual connection between the two men was rooted, in part, in their shared experiences, but the anchor of their relationship was a mutual understanding of the importance of the public role to be played by all persons of good will. Stevenson understood that intellectuals like MacLeish, who as both creative writer and scholar fits so well the broad definition of intellectual, I offered in Chap. 1, have a unique role to play in bringing to bear on public policy the many fruits of creative passion and intellectual analysis. Likewise, MacLeish knew that the best public servants were those who, if they themselves were not intellectuals, were at least as sensitive to the appeal to reason and reflection as they were to pragmatism of conventional politics. It was this mutual understanding, and the mutual respect that grew from it, that permeated their public and private relationships.

From the moment they met, the Stevenson-MacLeish association was viewed by both men as exceedingly special. The relationship was not unique because it was the only literary friendship forged by Stevenson, nor was it the sole political friendship nurtured by MacLeish. MacLeish had an intense affinity for Franklin Roosevelt and was devastated by his death in 1945 (see "April Elegy" in which MacLeish compares the deaths of Roosevelt and Lincoln). He also maintained a close relationship with Secretary of State Dean Acheson. In fact, Acheson was the public political figure with whom MacLeish probably was most intimate. Acheson and MacLeish were Harvard Law School classmates, and the Achesons were annual guests at the MacLeish's Caribbean winter retreat in Antigua for nearly twenty years. In R.H. Winnick's collection of MacLeish's correspondence, *Letters of Archibald MacLeish 1907–1982*, there are twenty-eight entries for Acheson, a mere ten for Stevenson (Winnick 451, 469). In Scott Donaldson's *Archibald MacLeish: An American Life* a similar split is recorded; thirty-six references for Acheson and only fifteen for Stevenson (Donaldson 601, 620).

Clearly, the Stevenson-MacLeish alliance was different in that MacLeish was attracted to Stevenson as an unusually literate politician (Stevenson appears in successive editions of *Benet's Readers Encyclopedia* while Acheson does not), and Stevenson was attracted to MacLeish as an unusually politically responsible intellectual.

Stevenson and MacLeish first met in Washington, D.C. in 1941, where both had enlisted in the multiple crusades of President Franklin Delano Roosevelt's administration. Stevenson had been in and out of the capital, appearing in an official capacity first as an assistant in the Agriculture

Department during the flowering of the New Deal and later as an assistant to the Secretary of the Navy.

At the time of their initial meeting MacLeish's official government role was as head of the Office of Facts and Figures, an organization which Roosevelt hoped would not mirror the ugly side of its World War I predecessor and propaganda machine, the Committee for Public Information (Blum 21). MacLeish seemed a good choice for such a position. He had "the humane sensibilities of a poet" (22), was Librarian of Congress, and was generally respected, although many intellectuals, as we shall see, felt that his political advocacy corrupted his art.

The MacLeish appointment, many thought, would prompt an outpouring of support for the war effort, but the impact was limited in this regard. However, The League of American Writers, which counted among its members Ernest Hemingway, Thorton Wilder, John Steinbeck, and MacLeish, and had as its President and Vice-President Dashiell Hammett and Erskine Caldwell, did encourage writers to serve the country with their talents and to contact MacLeish at the Office of Facts and Figures if they were willing to help (Schwartz 188). But, in the end, intellectuals were divided over United States' participation in the war. MacLeish eventually left the Office of Facts and Figures before it was transformed into the Office of War Information. His major objection to OFF was that the organization publicly defended the war because it protected an American way of life that, according to MacLeish, was smug and materialistic (Blum 23), not because the war was a legitimate ideological crusade against fascism.

MacLeish remained connected to the Roosevelt administration, willingly serving under the title of Assistant Secretary of State for Cultural Affairs, while Stevenson returned to Illinois to practice law in Chicago. But Stevenson had made an impression on MacLeish sufficient to prompt MacLeish to persuade Stevenson to return to Washington for work at the State Department. With MacLeish publicly describing Adlai Stevenson as "one of the most valuable men in all Washington" (Donaldson 382), and Secretary of State Edward Stettinius echoing the call, Stevenson consented, returning to the capital in late 1944.

Stevenson's working title at the State Department changed frequently. He was known first as "Special Assistant to Assistant Secretary Mr. MacLeish," then "Special Assistant to the Secretary," and next as "Deputy to Mr. Stettinius" (Martin 234). Revolving titles notwithstanding, the fact of the matter is that he was Archibald MacLeish's assistant! Professor

Donaldson cites a newspaper article of the time describing Stevenson as MacLeish's "right hand man" (Donaldson 270). Their offices were next to each other at the State Department and Stevenson biographer Kenneth Davis has written that daily contact between the two of them "cemented a permanent and mutually admiring friendship" (Davis 160).

Shortly after Stevenson joined him in Washington, MacLeish instructed his secretary: "Please tell Adlai Stevenson that I thank God for him every morning" (Donaldson 383). Even as the two were connected privately, observers of public affairs began to speak of MacLeish and Stevenson in the same breath. *The Chicago Daily News* reported that "MacLeish, with the valuable assistance of Adlai Stevenson of Chicago, is making the people of this country State Department conscious.... [They have] awakened public interest in the function of the State Department, which is to wage peace. It is no small tribute to the presence of Stevenson and MacLeish" (Johnson 2: 231). The MacLeish-Stevenson collaboration continued in writing the press release after Roosevelt's death in April of 1945 and at the formative meetings for the United Nations in San Francisco.

Soon after Truman was sworn in as President, MacLeish resigned as Assistant Secretary of State for Cultural Affairs and proposed Stevenson as his successor. Stevenson declined with the kind of humility and self-effacement that endeared him to intellectuals, writing to MacLeish: "I don't think I rate your job...I'm just a low order of country lawyer with a congenial taste for public service." In added flattery to his friend, Stevenson, as he did with other intellectuals, asked for a signed photograph of MacLeish (Donaldson 390).

In the immediate post-Roosevelt era, Stevenson returned to Illinois, MacLeish to poetry, but their bond was sustained and their paths would cross again. I return first to a principal part of this discussion, that of MacLeish as an intellectual "drenched in politics."

Archibald MacLeish suffered for his political activity. Typical of the suspicious was patron of the arts Gerald Murphy, who in a 1939 letter to his wife Sara wondered about MacLeish taking a job in Washington, writing: "Possibly he belongs to the state and not to poetry" (Donnelly 200). His fellow poets and critics frequently went beyond suspicion to a rather blatant ostracism. Representative of the extreme, as one might expect from their long-standing feud, was Edmund Wilson, who refused to shake hands with MacLeish when both were in a hospital room consoling John Dos Passos after his wife's tragic automobile accident in 1947 (391).

MacLeish's relationship with Wilson was broken irreparably by his [MacLeish's] open condemnation of Dos Passos, Hemingway, and others because "the books they wrote in the years just after the war [WW I] have done more to disarm democracy in the face of fascism than any other single influence" (Wilson 3). MacLeish additionally, and again openly, indicted his literary generation for educating the next "to believe that all declarations, all beliefs, are fraudulent" (Aaron 377). MacLeish's claim that many of his intellectual colleagues were irresponsible and "rendered impotent by their objectivity" (377) caused extensive damage to his association with many critics and artist-peers alike. Wilson retorted that MacLeish was the "real literary irresponsible" with his "jingoistic advocacy of international conflict" (Donaldson 336). Others joined the Wilson-led censure. Burton Rascoe, literary editor of the *New York Tribune*, called MacLeish "a would-be Fuhrer," while others referred to him as "Hitler's Poet Laureate" (337), and the critic and poet Louise Bogan said "he had dwindled into a mere propagandist" for the Roosevelt administration (351), and referred to him as "Mac Slush," while Bernard DeVoto's classification was "crisis patriot" (337).

Dwight Macdonald, whose own epithet for MacLeish was "patrioteer" (337) wrote that American intellectuals traditionally try to "find their way back to the long-discredited bourgeoisie, or else...move toward a totalitarian solution" (Macdonald, "Kulterbolsheivismus" 203). He certainly saw MacLeish as taking the first route: in effect "selling out" to the establishment. For Macdonald, Archibald MacLeish had allowed himself to be absorbed by a "middle brow counter-revolution" which believed that the avant-garde had lost touch with the people and was in a state of self-destructive superiority (Macdonald, *Against the American Grain* 208). James Farrell seemed to agree with Macdonald, calling MacLeish an "ideological policeman" and a "frightened Philistine" (Donaldson 337). Donald Donaldson and Allen Tate ridiculed MacLeish, even as Tate was offered a job, through MacLeish, at the Library of Congress. In the face of such criticism, it seems amazing that MacLeish remained kind to Wilson and Dos Passos, just as he had been kind to Ezra Pound when others abandoned him.

Other writers, like Malcolm Cowley, who had worked briefly (three months) for MacLeish at the Office of Facts and Figures, were more understanding of the dilemma for intellectuals who were moved to politics. Cowley called the temptation to serve the state, as MacLeish was doing, a disease; "but it is a disease" wrote Cowley, "to be honest with myself, I know I share, though with a great deal more self-consciousness and self-criticism" (Jay 244). Cowley acknowledged a conflict "between the private world of poets…and the world of public issues," with the poet thinking "in terms of individual persons and objects" and the public man dealing "with movements that affect the masses" (Donaldson 226). MacLeish could share such an acknowledgment, but as Professor Donaldson has pointed out, "MacLeish chose not to accept this as an unbreakable division" (226).

The evidence supporting Donaldson's view is incontrovertible when examined through both MacLeish's rhetoric and his actions. Early on MacLeish wrote to Dean Acheson that "it was a man's purpose to act upon the world, not to wait to see what the world will do to him;" that "an art which lives by the production of little books to lie on little tables is not an art in flower" (Marien 14).

With such rhetoric, Archibald MacLeish would continue to defend himself unabashedly in private, in public, and, of course, through his creations. In his often misunderstood "Invocation to The Social Muse" (1932), MacLeish beckons his intellectual peers, particularly poets, to bear the arms of social action. "Invocation" is frequently used as an indictment of MacLeish, an example of selling his soul to that worst of devils, the state. Yet in the poem MacLeish urges a turn away from any dogma, ridiculing both Karl Marx on the left and J.P. Morgan and Herbert Hoover on the right. In doing so, he merely encourages poets to engage thoughtfully political and social questions, to enter into forbidden territory and "mix in maneuvers." Likewise, in "Speech to The Scholars" (1937), a poem read at Phi Beta Kappa ceremonies at Columbia University, MacLeish exhorts: "Arise O Scholars from your peace! / Arise Enlist! Take Arms and Fight" (Donaldson 166).

Perhaps the most articulate defense of intellectuals participating more fully in public life came during a most revealing interview for the *Paris Review* in 1974. I quote quite liberally from it here because the remarks are not only vintage MacLeish but also represent the MacLeish that Adlai Stevenson found so attractive. Responding to questions about art and the public man MacLeish said:

> There are those on the fringes of art who think that poetry and the public world should be mutually exclusive…as though poets were the internists of the profession and should stick to their bowels…. You can't cut off a part of human life by critical fiat and expect your poets to be whole. Poetry is the

art of understanding what it is to be alive and a poet isn't alive by quarter-acres or front-feet. He's alive as a man.... One of the dimensions of great poetry...is precisely that public dimension: that vast landscape off beyond...the human background, total human background...what we call "the world." The Greeks regarded what we call "public" experience as part of *human* [emphasis mine] experience. That's what a man was: he was *a poet* [emphasis mine] who was a member of his city.... This is perhaps one way of answering the question: that a man who excludes ... the public part of his experience is apt to end up finding himself excluded. (DeMott 310–313)

Earlier, MacLeish had expressed all of this by way of a personal mandate for himself and fellow poet Carl Sandburg. "You and I," he wrote to Sandburg, "have considerable responsibility. We are poets but we are also men able to live in the world. We cannot escape our duty as political animals" (Marien 14). It is not surprising, then, to find that among MacLeish's favored writers were the poet-statesmen W.B. Yeats (previously mentioned), St.-John Perse and George Seferis (Donaldson x). Perse, the pen name of Alexis Saint-Leger Leger, was a French poet and diplomat who received the Nobel Prize for Literature in 1960. Unlike MacLeish, Perse labored to keep his true identities separate, in effect, leading double lives. Seferis, the pen name of George Seferiadis, was a Greek poet and diplomat who received the Nobel Prize for Literature in 1963 and was also the Greek Ambassador to England.

Archibald MacLeish was determined to live the "complete life" as he gleaned it from the ancient Greeks; life as an intellectual artist involved in the political issues of his day. So, too, Adlai Stevenson was committed to the "complete life;" life as a politician with literary interests and a keen regard for language. This commonality brought MacLeish and Stevenson together, sustained their friendship, and at the same time, aroused a certain suspicion of both men. Both their lives were propelled by seemingly incongruent goals. MacLeish "wanted to write great poetry and he also wanted to advance great causes" (Donaldson ix), to be a "rising politician" of sorts.

Stevenson wanted to raise the level of political discourse to a higher moral plane, even as he wanted to devote substantial time to the meticulous architecture of words as a "would be" writer. In short, just as MacLeish disdained purists in the intellectual world, Stevenson disdained the purists in the political world. In return, the purists in both worlds harbored suspicion of them and questioned their vocational effectiveness.

To be sure, MacLeish's and Stevenson's heritage and upbringing fostered their attitudes of respect for both literature and politics. A look at MacLeish's earliest years, in fact, reveals a pattern in childhood reminiscent of Stevenson's discussed in an earlier chapter. As for Adlai Stevenson, it was the mother who daily read to him from the great literature; Homer, Rudyard Kipling, Walter Scott, and Geoffrey Chaucer (17). Donaldson describes Martha Hillard MacLeish as having "a quick mind, extraordinary felicity of language, and a forward-looking, turn-of-the-century, middle western optimism" (x). His mother encouraged the son to become classically literate and socially responsible. The heritage of respect for formal learning found in the Stevenson lineage also was found in the MacLeish's. MacLeish's mother was President of Rockford Seminary and his father served on the Board of Trustees at the University of Chicago (18).

Other similarities emerge in a comparison as well: both MacLeish and Stevenson had a penchant for travel that seemed insatiable, and both struggled with self-doubt. Still, it is the double lives they so willingly led which provided the dynamic of their relationship. In a post-publication interview, biographer Donaldson said that MacLeish "felt an obligation to make poetry do the work of politics." A lot of people were turned off by that. From an aesthetic end it was said his poetry became propaganda. From the political end MacLeish was seen as an interloper" (Cattani 19). The same can be said of Stevenson. He felt an obligation to make politics an acceptable medium for the passion of language. A lot of people were turned off by that. From a political end it was said that he cared more about writing and delivering "literary" speeches than succeeding in the grit of governing. Regarding MacLeish, Donaldson's conclusion that "in adopting a public persona, he had almost lost track of himself" (19) is a valid one. But in the last analysis, it is not the only conclusion to be drawn from a careful look at MacLeish's life. I believe that for both Stevenson and MacLeish the adoption of a persona that seemed to many of their contemporaries as incompatible with vocational and professional patterns did not translate into "losing track" of themselves at all. Quite the opposite occurred. MacLeish only found himself and kept track of himself by being the public poet, socially committed and socially relevant. In a similar fashion, Stevenson only found and kept track of himself by reflectively laboring over his speeches and letters until satisfied that they had achieved literary quality. A truly "lost" MacLeish was one retreating to the world of letters without regard for "acting upon the world." A truly "lost"

Stevenson was one wrapped in electioneering without regard for the beauty and grace of words and the company of those who wrote them. When MacLeish tried to lure Stevenson to Washington in January of 1945, he sought him out because of the shared world-view that gave equal emphasis to the head and the heart. MacLeish: "I need the assistance and the counsel and the collaboration and the advice of a man who believes what you [and I] believe, who sees problems as you [and I] see them" and

> I have felt since the days of the Committee on War information that you were one of the most valuable men in this Government. I have felt that, not on the basis of personal affection...though the personal affection exists...but on the basis of observation and experience. In that difficult, confused, and rather desperate first year of the war, there were about a dozen men in Washington who seemed to me to be irreplaceable. You were one of them. I felt at the time that your resignation from Government was a disaster. I feel the same thing now. (Winnick 326)

MacLeish's letter reflected the mutual respect that permeated virtually all correspondence between the two men. As I have pointed out already, such two-way flattery between intellectuals and Stevenson was pervasive; yet there is something between MacLeish and Stevenson that seems more potently endearing and personal.

Consider this, for example, from Stevenson to MacLeish in August of 1949: "I yearn for you, and should the Boyleston Professor at Harvard [MacLeish's position at the time] want to dig his fingers into the roots, I will provide the roots. My love to you both [MacLeish and wife Ada]" (Johnson 3: 141).

And for Stevenson's part, even in the throes of an unfolding Presidential campaign, he deferred to MacLeish's accolades and encouraged his literary quests with "May the sun shine and the poems bloom" (527). Presumably, a Presidential candidate would have no time to embolden writers. Stevenson made time.

In July of 1952, MacLeish began drafting speeches for his old acquaintance, writing to Stevenson: "I am at your service, typewriter, yellow pad and all...God bless you my dear friend" (Johnson 4: 22). Later that month, a flattered and self-effacing Stevenson replied: "Anything you say is much better than I could say it...just write your way" (43).

In the wake of Stevenson's defeat that autumn, MacLeish joined countless other intellectuals in offering words of despair, or thanks, or

encouragement, or a combination of all three. Stevenson graciously responded to such letters and to the MacLeishes he did so with unusually warm and deeply personal expressions.
My beloved MacLeishes:

> Your wire lifted my heart. As a matter of fact, my heart seems to be much higher than my friends' hearts! I have no regrets except their disappointment.
>   I shall not be able to thank you for the literature you contributed to my public offerings, but I think you know how I feel. We shall live to fight another day. Affectionately, Adlai (199)

Six weeks after the election, the MacLeishes invited Stevenson to visit them at their winter home on Antigua, in the West Indies. Here, too, one sees a MacLeish intonation that is more endearing, more urgent, more deeply felt than most of the other intellectuals' communication with Stevenson. "We simply won't take no for an answer," wrote MacLeish, "We'll be strident and unmannerly. And why? Because we love you, long to see you, and can think of no place on earth where seeing you would be pleasanter" (Winnick 363).

By the mid-1950s, the friendship had matured to the point that Stevenson was inviting himself to stay with the MacLeishes at their home in Cambridge, Massachusetts! Inquires Stevenson: "Will you and Ada be in Cambridge [at the time of Stevenson's trip to the East], and if so, could I beg a bed for Saturday night, February 12, and just possibly Sunday as well?" (Johnson 4: 451). The MacLeishes "accepted" on that occasion and Stevenson's thank you note carried the, by now, characteristic affection: "My Dearly Beloved! Somehow there is always light and warmth and a little magic about your menages...and I shall be back!" (453).

Intertwined with the special and purely personal fondness for MacLeish, was Stevenson's sincere appreciation for MacLeish's political and editorial assistance. As he approached the Presidential campaign of 1956, Stevenson asked MacLeish for input in formulating policy statements, telling him that few of his friends "can be truly helpful in the way you have always been" (538). In such requests, as in the thanks for services rendered, Stevenson was bursting with praise for MacLeish's prodigious literary talent, writing in late 1955 that a MacLeish-penned draft of a speech was "beautiful, superb!...and much too good for this week's AFL-CIO convention I think...good in the sober, thoughtful, literary sense" (Johnson

6: 11). Stevenson's critics are apt to cite such a statement as further evidence that he was arrogant, even condescending, toward the blue-collar wing of the Democratic Party. Perhaps, but what is clearly true is that beneath the praise in this particular case is Stevenson's recognition that in politics, to be too literate, too delicate in language can be a liability. Stevenson admitted to such a struggle in a letter to MacLeish the following August: "I find it awfully hard to write to win, rather than writing to say what you feel is important" (201).

With his second Presidential bid foiled in 1956, Stevenson's Presidential political future was most likely sealed; only William Jennings Bryan secured his party's nomination a third time after twice losing in the general election (1896, 1900, 1908). Thus, his contribution to public life took new and various forms. As titular leader of the Democratic Party, his was the mantle to pass on to a new generation and he was kept busy speaking and writing about the future. By 1959, MacLeish complained about not having the chance to see Stevenson enough: "You and I haven't really had so much as an hour together...to be quite frank about it...I miss you" (Winnick 416).

Stevenson's ill-fated and ill-timed move for a third consecutive nomination in 1960 rekindled his connection to many intellectuals, but it was MacLeish and, as I shall point out in the next chapter, John Steinbeck, to whom Stevenson turned as a primary nexus. In a long, sometimes rambling letter to MacLeish after the Democratic National Convention in Los Angeles, Stevenson maintained at least two of the components in his attraction to intellectuals in general; a letter which ends, importantly, with a personal reference to his close friend. Referring to his letter, Stevenson wrote:

> If you wish to drop this in the wastebasket, please do so. And certainly, don't let me intrude beyond your own interest in either time or energy. My position of intellectual and oratorical bankruptcy is perpetual, but sometimes even that is now wholly apparent to the audiences...and I don't want to impose, especially on incorrigible friends. (Johnson 7: 556)

Here again, one sees Stevenson in self-effacing humility and also in reverence to MacLeish's artistic labors by not wanting to "intrude." What interests me, too, is Stevenson's lamentation for his fleeting (as he saw it) intellectual and oratorical skills.

I sense that the fear of losing his ability to articulately present an idea, or to "turn a phrase" was more formidable for him than losing any purely political power he may have had. A pure politician, significantly less attractive to intellectuals, would not have been bothered to the degree that he was by such growing inadequacies.

During the months before Stevenson's death, correspondence to MacLeish reveals a sustained and abiding personal friendship. Stevenson wrote to MacLeish: "I wish to God, I saw you" (Johnson 8: 425), and "I wish, I wish, I wish you were coming to New York" (579). A few months after this last letter, MacLeish, in fact, did go to New York; not to engage Stevenson's company, but to memorialize him at the United Nations. What he said that mid-summer day strikes me as the epitome of why Stevenson was the darling of the intellectuals. His remarks also bear testament to the strong personal feelings MacLeish had for Stevenson. Moreover, that he was asked to address the General Assembly in the first place indicates that their special relationship was acknowledged by the entire world. MacLeish proclaimed:

> Works of will are notoriously short-lived and even works of intellect can fail when the intelligence is cynical or dry. It is only when the end is reached through the human heart as well as through the human mind that the accomplishment is sure to endure. And it is for that reason that Adlai Stevenson seems certain of remembrance…. His great achievement was the enrichment of his time by the nature of his relationship with his time. If his intelligence was remarkable, it was remarkable even more for its clarity, for its modesty, its humor, its naturalness, its total lack of vanity or arrogance…one of the great articulators of his time…. It was himself he gave in word and thought and action, not to his friends alone but to the country, to his world. (vii)

Had fate been different, it is conceivable that these words, so full of passion, could have been uttered by Adlai Stevenson in memory of Archibald MacLeish. MacLeish, too, possessed the rare balance of heart and head. And Stevenson surely would have said of MacLeish that he gave in word and thought, and, significantly for the theme of this work, that he gave in action as well. He "gave not to his friends alone, but to his country."

Nobel Prize winner John Steinbeck in 1962

Adlai Stevenson and John Steinbeck

Abstract Chapter 6 is the second of the case studies used to bolster the premise that although Stevenson had an enduring and endearing relationship with many literary intellectuals, some, like that with John Steinbeck were remarkably close.

Keywords Intimacy • Sensibility • Internationalism • Self-doubt • Inspiration

> *The "Stevenson Letters" will be my most precious legacy to literature, to political science, to history…and my children…You lift my heart.*
> —Stevenson to Steinbeck (Johnson 7: 518)
>
> *The sadness is for us who have lost our chance for greatness when greatness is needed…. It has been an honor to work for you…and a privilege…. Yours in disappointment and hope.*
> —Steinbeck to Stevenson (Steinbeck, _Letters_ 461)

John Steinbeck and Adlai Stevenson knew each other for only thirteen years. During that time, however, their relationship was marked by the same kind of intellectual and moral intimacy discussed in the previous chapter. Like the Stevenson-MacLeish association, that between Stevenson

C. B. Bultman, _Adlai E. Stevenson and American Intellectuals_, https://doi.org/10.1007/978-3-031-80648-3_6

and Steinbeck was cemented in mutual respect and admiration, and in the shared judgment that politics and literature not only can mix, but ought to.

Steinbeck's and Stevenson's lives actually ran a closer chronological parallel than that of MacLeish and Stevenson's. Steinbeck was born in 1902 and died in 1968, and Stevenson was born in 1900 and died in 1965. As was the case with MacLeish and Stevenson, these congruent life cycles afforded a world-view shaped by vast wars and great depression. But the Steinbeck-Stevenson connection, like that of MacLeish and Stevenson, was much more than calendar based. To be sure, Steinbeck saw the same Stevenson that MacLeish did; a politician with poet-like sensibilities and the flexible mind of an intellectual. Similarly, Stevenson saw in Steinbeck what he saw in Archibald MacLeish; to revisit Vaclav Havel, the special existence of a writer "drenched in politics."

In the previous chapter I noted that Archibald MacLeish's friendship with Adlai Stevenson was not the only one that moved him [MacLeish] from the world of literature to the world of politics. His work in the Roosevelt administration and his long-time personal relationship with Dean Acheson remains the best example of that. John Steinbeck, likewise, had political ties other than to Stevenson throughout his life; first to Franklin Delano Roosevelt in the 1940s and then to Lyndon Baines Johnson in the 1960s. I attempt, here, to affirm the earlier point; that despite these other relationships, the one held between Steinbeck and Stevenson was uniquely personal and serves as further evidence that Adali Stevenson endeared himself to intellectuals like no other politician of his time. Irving Howe: "Roosevelt was to be admired for things he had done. Stevenson was to be admired and identified with simply because what he was" (Howe, "Stevenson," 3).

First, a look at Steinbeck and Roosevelt. Over fifty years ago, in an article for *The Politics of Twentieth Century Novelists*, professor, author, and editor Warren French claimed that "Except during Adlai Stevenson's campaigns for the Presidency, John Steinbeck was reluctant to commit himself to political positions" (French 296). French also reminded his readers that it was actually Eleanor Roosevelt, not her husband, who first brought Steinbeck to the White House. In the summer of 1939, Mrs. Roosevelt had praised Steinbeck's newly published *The Grapes of Wrath* in her syndicated newspaper column. The recognition that followed prompted an invitation to the throne of American political power in September of the following year (296).

The friendship that ensued was based, in part, on shared ideology. Steinbeck novels such as *Tortilla Flat* (1935), *In Dubious Battle* (1936), and *The Grapes of Wrath* (1939), all reflect, at the very least, Steinbeck's acute interest in the world's dispossessed, an interest shared by the Roosevelts.

Steinbeck's White House visit in 1940 established enough of a tie to bring him back into contact with Roosevelt during the Presidential campaign of 1944. The depth and breadth of his involvement is open to debate. Researcher Clifford Lewis, in an engaging and informative article about Steinbeck's support for Franklin Roosevelt's fourth and final run for the Presidency, argues that two Steinbeck-penned documents were central to the core of the President's mid-decade policies. One was a letter from Steinbeck to administration officials which, according to Lewis, provided material for a subsequent letter from the President to the Chairman of the Democratic National Committee, Robert Hannegan, outlining several reasons why Roosevelt should most definitely seek re-election. The other document was a statement of eleven principles which Lewis asserts are clearly evident in Roosevelt's acceptance speech, and through which he sets forth his goals for the next four years (Lewis 195). Clearly, the documents "contradict statements that argue Steinbeck was neither committed to a political movement nor intellectual enough to formulate a political ideology" (192). The documents reveal a Steinbeck swept up by, and contributing to, New Deal liberalism through the presentation of ideas. But do they say anything more?

Lewis uses these two pre-national nominating convention proposals to show that Steinbeck's "argument for a fourth term became FDR's" (196), and makes references to the "Steinbeck-Roosevelt team" (204). Admittedly, the two men were close personal friends. But Lewis's claim, it seems to me, stretches their relationship beyond what it was for either man. Steinbeck's involvement in the Roosevelt administration was limited and extremely private. Even Lewis admits (in a footnote) that Steinbeck "may have asked privately to keep the campaign work a secret, so that it would not interfere with the reception of his fiction" (215). Two draft proposals, forwarded in secrecy, and most likely never seen in the original by Roosevelt himself, do not strike me as unusual, open political advocacy and personal loyalty, any more than the whole affair warrants the label "team." If Clifford Lewis's criticism of Steinbeck biographer Jackson J. Bensen for making no references at all to Steinbeck's work for FDR (194) has merit, then so, too, does criticism of Lewis for attempting to make much of little. Was Steinbeck alert to presidential politics before Stevenson came into his life? Most certainly. Lewis's article validates that much. But any effort to equate Steinbeck's interest in the re-election of

Franklin Roosevelt with the intensity of his later relationship with Stevenson would be a mistake.

Much also has been made of Steinbeck's association with Lyndon Baines Johnson. During the mid-1960s, he, indeed, was courted by the President. That Steinbeck ever felt "used" by Johnson remains uncertain, though Bensen writes that LBJ

> saw in John some political advantage. As a Stevenson supporter, John had ties with a wing of the Democratic Party that had been hostile to Johnson; as a Nobel Prize winner and author whose books were beloved by many readers, he would be a useful figure to have associated with his presidency; and as an accomplished writer with some speechwriting experience...he could become a valuable resource for a President, who must, perforce, try to communicate effectively with the general public. (Bensen 957)

One should also be reminded at this point that it was a relatively easy decision even for otherwise non-partisan, apolitical intellectuals to become involved in presidential politics in 1964. Since Johnson's opponent was Republican Senator Barry Goldwater of Arizona, the standard-bearer of the right wing, Steinbeck and others found compelling reasons for activism. Goldwater's bellicose rhetoric and his apparent intolerance of almost everything except the most extreme ideological positions frightened many academic and creative intellectuals into political mobilization.

The sometimes-lavish treatment of Steinbeck was probably the result of both personal and political considerations on the part of the President. The Steinbecks were flown in and out of Washington in military planes sent by Johnson, and when staying at the White House they were attended "almost like members of the family.... They stayed near the Johnsons on the second floor in the Queen's Bedroom...and were able to have breakfast in the little office where Lincoln often breakfasted" (957). Even when Steinbeck was at his home at Sag Harbor, on Long Island, Johnson took extraordinary steps to make Steinbeck's political contributions convenient, sending drafts of speeches for him to work on by military plane. Steinbeck's wife, Elaine, admitted the lure of the center of power and often said to her husband, "You'd better get me out of here [Washington, D.C.]...I'm getting to like this too much" (957).

Johnson's treatment of Steinbeck was, no doubt, a form of appreciation for his active support of the President. Acclaim for such support came in liberal doses.

Steinbeck and Russion-born composer Igor Stravinsky headed the "National Committee of The Arts, Letters, and Humanities for Johnson and Humphrey," and Steinbeck was later appointed to the National Arts Council (French 297). Like Mrs. Steinbeck, John Steinbeck did not resist either the personal or public acknowledgments; he "had an inordinate respect for the office of the presidency and was vulnerable to the excitement and flattery that came from being around a president, feeling the history and majesty of the White House on an intimate basis" (Bensen 957).

Despite Steinbeck's closeness to Lyndon Johnson and the trappings of political power, according to biographer Bensen, he remained skeptical about the President: "He viewed him with much the same suspicion common to most liberals...as a too conservative Democrat, who in the Senate was a wheeler-dealer with too much willingness to compromise" (957). Steinbeck's skepticism also applied to U.S. conduct of the war in Vietnam.

Even though Steinbeck publicly supported Johnson's policy, a view probably intensified by his own son's participation in the war, he privately agonized over it. To Mr. and Mrs. Jack Valenti he admitted that there was "no way to make the Vietnamese War decent" and "no way of justifying sending troops to another man's country," adding that the government Johnson was supporting in the South was "about as smelly as you can get" (Steinbeck, *Letters* 826).

John Steinbeck may have hoped for, even sought, recognition and power through his relationship with President Johnson, but he seems to have sought something much more in his ties with Adlai Stevenson. In the thirteen years that Steinbeck knew him, Stevenson never did hold a position of vast and obvious political power. Yet, they had as close an association as politician and writer could expect to have, and more.

In the beginning it was public words that fostered the intersection of men in such different occupations; by the end, it was public *and private* words that bonded their relationship. They were genuinely fond of each other, and when they were together, they were able, in the words of e. e. cummings, to be nobody but themselves in a world laboring day and night to make them everybody else (Farber 1965).

Steinbeck's political support for Stevenson seems to have come rather abruptly. In fact, originally, he had been attracted to Eisenhower's presidential candidacy in 1952. Since Steinbeck had been a war correspondent in both Europe and Africa, he was no doubt not exempt from the draw of Eisenhower's crusade-like leadership and his ubiquitous and affable smile. Steinbeck recalled that in 1951 he had never even heard of Adlai Stevenson and a short time later only remembered him because of that unusual first name (Marovitz 118). Further, Steinbeck admitted that "until the convention I had never heard nor read a Stevenson word," but since the convention "we hurry through dinner to hear him on the radio or see him on television. We fight over the morning paper with the full text," adding that he "couldn't remember ever reading a political speech with pleasure – with admiration, yes, but never with pleasure" (Steinbeck, Speeches 5).

Steinbeck's original attraction to Stevenson turned quickly to allegiance after he became more familiar with Stevenson's campaign speeches. In the foreword to *Speeches of Adlai Stevenson* Steinbeck wrote:

> I have switched entirely because of the speeches.... A man cannot think muddled and write clear. Day by day it has seemed to me that Eisenhower's speeches have become more formless and mixed up and uncertain.... As a writer I love the clean, clear writing of Stevenson. As a man I like his intelligent, humorous, logical, civilized mind. (Steinbeck, *Speeches* 5)

Like many other intellectuals, Steinbeck pleaded with Stevenson to run again in 1956. Just two months after the 1952 defeat, *The New Republic* published an open letter from Steinbeck to Stevenson in which he wrote: "You have given us a look at truth as a weapon, at reason as a tool, at humor as a method, and at democracy as a particular way of life. We would be crazy to let you go," concluding with "your greatness is the property of the nation" (Steinbeck, "The Sevenson Spirit"). pp. 333–334).

So solid was the switch that Steinbeck, who once described himself as a "New Deal Democrat," defined himself now and for the rest of his life as a "Stevenson Democrat" (Bensen 734). John Steinbeck's respect for words, for Adlai Stevenson's words in particular, worked its way into letters to Stevenson and about Stevenson. But it also worked its way into some of Steinbeck's novels.

In *The Winter of Our Discontent* (1961), Steinbeck's Ethan Hawley recalls his Aunt Deborah's insistence on precision in expression: "She cared deeply about words and she hated their misuse as she would hate the clumsy handling of any fine thing" (Steinbeck, *Winter* 216). Additionally, and in the same novel, Steinbeck could not resist accentuating the contrast, as he saw it, between Stevenson and Eisenhower on the "handling of" words. When Ethan's son, Allen, earns Honorable Mention for his entry in an essay contest, he remarks: "I'm just astonished. I thought his prose style was about the level of General Eisenhower's" (259). It seems neither incidental, nor accidental, that Steinbeck's inclusion of such musings in a novel born of the fifties and published in the early sixties paralleled an intensified friendship with Adlai Stevenson.

A Stevenson to Steinbeck letter in August of 1960, in which Stevenson asked for help with an article he was writing, reveals first, Stevenson's acknowledgment of Steinbeck's themes in *The Winter of Our Discontent* (a materialistic, spiritless, empty existence and national leadership to match), and second, that ever-present Stevenson humility in his relationship with intellectuals.

Stevenson:

> It sounds to me as though 'the winter of our discontent" is on the same theme. If you could find time to give me a few reflections, I would be gratified indeed. I suspect, however, that this is a pretty lighthearted discussion and hardly worthy of your thoughts. So, if I hear nothing I shall not be surprised. (Johnson 7:561)

Imagine a two-time major party presidential candidate not expecting to hear from anyone because he [Stevenson] may not be "worthy"!

Earlier, in what most critics consider a light treatment of the American political mood of the 1950s, Steinbeck seems more directly to bring Stevenson to life in fiction. *The Short Reign of Pippin IV* (1957), set in France, is the story of Pippin Arnulf Heristal's elevation to the French throne. As one reads about Pippin's ascendancy and the brief reign that follows, parallels to Stevenson and the intellectual community that so welcomed his rise to power became clear. Additionally, Steinbeck was rewriting *Pippin* during the Democratic National Convention in 1956, at which Stevenson gained the nomination for the second time.

Whether Stevenson saw himself in Pippin's fictional circumstances as clearly as others saw him there is uncertain. What we do know is that when Steinbeck informed him that his publisher was forwarding a copy of this, his latest book, Stevenson was delighted. He vowed to "cart it [*Pippin*] off with me on a forthcoming holiday and read it eagerly, gaily, and approvingly, I know" (Johnson 6: 418). Even if Stevenson did not anticipate the connection to his own life experiences, he did look forward enthusiastically to reading a new novel by John Steinbeck.

Stevenson's own critical judgment notwithstanding, there are unmistakable parallels to his public experience in Steinbeck's satire. Returning, for example, to the respect for Stevenson's literate manner, the reader finds that when Pippin senses failure, he laments, "I suppose I have failed." Sister Hyacinth's response to Pippin is instructive. "I don't know," she questions, "I have read your remarks to the convention. They were bold remarks, Sire. Yes, I imagine that you have failed, you personally, but I wonder whether your words have failed" (*Pippin* 179). In a tone reminiscent of some Stevenson critics, Pippin's wife accusingly suggests that Pippin "just sits around reading" (66).

Embedded in the "I suppose I have failed" passage one also sees those Stevenson qualities of self-doubt and reluctance to assume power. Earlier in the novel Pippin exclaims, "I don't want to be King" (53); and after taking power he admonishes himself: "I can't imagine how I let myself in for this" (77). Pippin felt like

> a rat in a laboratory maze, sought every possible avenue of escape, explored runways and aisles and holes, only to run against the iron netting of fact. Again and again, he butted his mental nose against the screen at the end of a promising passage, and there was the fact. He was king...there was no escaping it. (55)

Steinbeck tapped vintage Stevenson with such exchanges and soliloquies. In Stevenson's acceptance speech at the Democratic National Convention in Chicago, on July 26, 1952, for example, he said; "I should have preferred to hear those words [acceptance of the nomination] uttered by a stronger, a wiser man than myself...I have asked the Merciful Father...the Father of us all...to let this cup pass from me" (Johnson 4: 16). Anticipating a convention draft the previous March, Stevenson wrote to theologian Reinhold Niebuhr, "I pray that I can measure up to that *horror* [emphasis mine] if it should ever come" (Johnson 3: 538). I remind the reader that to intellectuals, self-doubt and reluctance were not just negative characteristics, they were attributes in the most positive sense.

Among other Stevenson qualities alluring to intellectuals and exposed in *Pippin* was Stevenson's reflective nature. Warren French has written that Steinbeck, for one, hoped the direction of the country "might at last be entrusted to a quiet, introspective, cautiously idealist man" (French 297). Steinbeck chose astronomy for Pippin's hobby; a hobby which was "carried on at night and silently," adding that "the passions of astronomy, however, are no less profound because they are not noisy" (Pippin 12). No evidence exists that Adlai Stevenson was particularly interested in celestial mechanics or gazing at Shakespeare's "blessed candles of the night." Yet, he was not a noisy man in the noisy business of politics. Inasmuch as Stevenson at least verbalized his desire to avoid the din of electioneering, intellectuals were impressed.

Steinbeck's hope for an "idealistic man" as a national leader, as well as the pitfalls in such an assignment also are explored in *Pippin* dialogue. One character asks Pippin, "Aren't you going to have some difficulty being king?" Before he can answer, his daughter interjects with: "He is already. He not only wants to be above everything, every human weakness...He wants everybody to be good...and people just aren't good" (*Pippin* 101).

Furthermore, as he did with *The Winter of Our Discontent*, Steinbeck used *Pippin* to emphasize the overall political-social conditions which intellectuals found so deplorable in the 1950s. Such conditions were sufficiently deplorable, they thought, to seek a Pippin, or a Stevenson, as the hope for a brighter future. In the novel, France stood at a crossroads and was "under the tattered flag of the unwashed, the greedy, and the inept" (35). And

> consider the intellectuals, the dried-up minds. The writers in the past burned the name 'France' on the world. Now they were sitting in huddled misery, building a philosophy of despair, while the painters, with few exceptions, paint apathy and jealous anarchy. (138)

The intellectuals in Pippin's France "demanded his instant acceptance of the throne for the safety and future of France" (46) and perhaps as an avenue to their own resurgence. In Steinbeck's America intellectuals demanded no less from Adlai Stevenson.

In concluding his book *Steinbeck and Film* (1983), Joseph R. Millichap wrote that "Steinbeck's best fictions always picture a paradise lost, but posit a future paradise to be regained," and praised Steinbeck for celebrating "the great hope which underlies the building of human potential" (Millichap 178). Millichap's interpretation is not only helpful in the analysis of Steinbeck's close relationship with Stevenson, it is instructive for the more general theme of this work; that of the relationship between Stevenson and most of his intellectual supporters. As was discussed in an earlier chapter, the reasons for Stevenson as a *cause célèbres* among intellectuals are myriad and their view of him as "the great hope" and the conduit to a "future paradise to be regained" should certainly be included.

Was Stevenson Stenbeck's conduit to something else on the road to "paradise"? A conduit to personal prestige and power perhaps? If the answer is yes, such reasoning would hold that Steinbeck's association with Stevenson was nothing more than a repeat of the White House liaison of the 1940s and a preview of the red-carpet treatment by Lyndon Johnson in the 1960s. Like any human, Steinbeck probably enjoyed the trappings of public influence, and there is some evidence that this was true of his ties to Stevenson. For example, although Steinbeck never directly wrote for Stevenson the candidate in either the 1952 or 1956 campaigns, he did contribute ideas for speeches on several occasions (Benson 794) and surely felt his status elevated when Stevenson used them. Similarly, after the 1952 campaign, Steinbeck traveled throughout Europe for *Collier's* and was impressed by the degree to which European literary activity was fueled by politics. Once back in the United States, and in contact with Stevenson about the trip, he was asked by Stevenson to prepare advice on European affairs should he run for president again (Kiernan 303). Steinbeck was flattered. Later on, in 1961, with presidential aspirations presumably gone, Stevenson was appointed by President Kennedy as United States Ambassador to the United Nations; an occasion which seemed to delight Steinbeck more than Stevenson. He was privately excited at the prospect of having access to international debate via his friend (312).

As was the case with Archibald MacLeish, Steinbeck's proximity to political power came at a cost. Many of his fellow writers were suspicious that Steinbeck's political intimacy had smothered his creative voice. Amidst the distractions by the affairs of state, Steinbeck's works had become weak. At times, the criticism by his American literary peers was vicious. Fitzgerald in 1940: "He's a rather cagy cribber. Most of us began as imitators but it is something else for a man of his years and reputation to steal a whole scene as he did in 'Mice and Men'" (Bruccoli 612); Faulkner in 1957: [He is] "a newspaperman, not really a writer" (Karl 908); and Hemingway in 1959; "I could give him [Hemingway's publisher] a book every year like Steinbeck composed of my toenail parings" (Baker 893).

Some of the criticism, of course, was legitimately literary; Steinbeck was simply an irrelevant voice, said critics. And some of the criticism was rooted in jealousy. Steinbeck, after all, had flirted with politics while publishing nineteen books between 1939 and 1966; he won a Pulitzer Prize near the beginning of that span (1940) and the Nobel Prize for Literature near the end of it (1962). But much of the criticism argued that Steinbeck, like MacLeish, was nothing more than a detoured politician. As early as 1942, Edmund Wilson questioned whether 'the artistic and intellectual importance of the social-consciousness that mounted during the thirties" was not over estimated; and whether MacLeish and Steinbeck (and Robert Sherwood) weren't "really second-rate, even third-rate writers" (Wilson 385). But what seemed to incite Wilson's wrath the most was the possibility that writers close to political power and institutions "could turn out to...represent merely the beginning of some awful collectivist cant which will turn into official propaganda...I shouldn't trust the Steinbecks" (385). These are not surprising remarks from someone who for the last three decades of his life was to call politics "unsavory" (Douglas 167) and "diseased" (189). Thirty years later, drama scholar Robert Brustein, would agree, at least in part, writing that "something very odd happens even to the most idiosyncratic individuals when they are forced to act in an official capacity" (Brustein 160). Brustein was responding to a trip to the then Soviet Union by John Steinbeck and the playwright Edward Albee, where they were to engage Soviet officials and scholars in a discussion on "The American Way of Life" (160).

Steinbeck, like MacLeish, was sometimes attacked from both sides, not only in the debate over the propriety of a writer's acting in an "official capacity," but also in the debate over how much politics should drive art itself. Joseph Henry Jackson, in his introduction to *The Short Novels of John Steinbeck* (1953), singled out *In Dubious Battle* (1936) in this regard, writing that "In the 1930s some wanted him [Steinbeck] to go further than he did with politics. Some felt that he went too far and forsook literature" (Jackson ix).

Jackson Bensen has pointed out that Steinbeck himself was not oblivious to the dangers inherent in the political activism of literary and academic intellectuals. He voiced this suspicion to John Kenneth Galbraith when Galbraith was named ambassador to India by President Kennedy. Galbraith recalls being warned by Steinbeck that "No writer, teacher, nor man of required independence of mind had any business becoming an ambassador…It wasn't that I [Galbraith] would louse up the job or dislike it. Rather, I would like it too much" (Bensen 958). In the case of Steinbeck's support for the presidential bids and the ensuing ambassadorship of Stevenson, he was more than willing to risk liking "it too much."

Yet no other politician, with or without power, could have been what Stevenson was to Steinbeck. In 1960 Steinbeck objected to candidates John Kennedy and Hubert Humphrey, not on ideological grounds, but because they were not Stevenson. There was too much empty rhetoric and no inspiration. When some intellectuals supported Kennedy that year, Steinbeck publicly helped organize academics and writers into a draft-Stevenson maneuver and chaired the advisory council to the Stevenson for President Committee of New York (Bensen 877).

To be sure, Steinbeck reconciled with Kennedy, admiring as did many, his grace and wit; and, as I have pointed out, he reconciled with Johnson as well. Even so, he always longed for Stevenson in the White House. On more than one occasion in the Oval Office, President Johnson asked, "You really wanted Adlai Stevenson in this office, didn't you, John?" (957). The answer was always "yes." During one of those exchanges, when Johnson added, "are you sorry?" Steinbeck responded: "Mr. President, that's water under the bridge. I can't tell you whether he would have made a good President or not. I think he might have" (958). Stevenson was simply irreplaceable. Neither power, nor prestige, nor appointments, nor White House hospitality was enough to erase from Steinbeck's mind what might have been.

Their private correspondence, as well as their shared private moments, indicates that Steinbeck and Stevenson's junction was more than political. At the 1956 Democratic National Convention in Chicago, Stevenson pulled Steinbeck into an ante-room and said, "'Sit down, I need a drink. The two sat talking for a half hour.... Every time he got up to go, Stevenson asked him to stay. It was the first time in days, Stevenson told him, that he had had a chance to relax" (794). Several weeks later, Stevenson wrote to Steinbeck: "Bless you and many thanks. I am still indignant that I had no more time with you in Chicago. I am putting 'Atavism and Old Lace' aside for the bed table tonight" (Johnson 6: 209). That the Steinbeck piece remains unidentifiable is less important than that the letter itself is evidence of the deeply felt regret at not being able to be together. No less important for this work is that one sees again a Stevenson planning to read a Steinbeck draft during the heat of a presidential campaign! The frustration of having too little time with each other continued. In 1962 Stevenson seemed to beg for the kind of companionship afforded only by his special literary friends. He wrote to Steinbeck in England: "When are you coming home? How long am I expected to survive this desert?" (Johnson 8: 239).

Their repining at not having a "chance to relax" together was quieted somewhat in the aftermath of Stevenson's defeat in 1956. Steinbeck visited Stevenson at the Libertyville farm, and later was frequently a guest in the Ambassador's Suite at the Waldorf Towers in New York City. Likewise, Steinbeck hosted Stevenson in Paris and at Steinbeck's home in Bruton, Somerset, in the Brae River Valley of England. Whenever they were together, they shared stories, discussed Arthurian legends and other Camelot mythology and expressed their mutual disdain for Richard Nixon, both believing that he was "the greatest threat to the Republic" (Bensen 836). It was Adlai Stevenson, the concerned friend, not Adlai Stevenson, the politician, who suggested to Steinbeck that the road trip that would become *Travels With Charley* (1962) would be "tonic for his [Steinbeck's] spiritual despair" (Millichap 164).

Adali Stevenson died on July 14, 1965. Two days later Steinbeck wrote to Lyndon Johnson's Press Secretary, Jack Valenti: "These are sad days. Adlai Stevenson was a great man and my friend. My first reaction to his death was one of rage that Americans had been too stupid to avail themselves of his complete ability" (*Letters* 825). Two weeks after Stevenson's death Steinbeck continued to express acute sadness in his correspondence. To his life-long friend, Carlton A. Sheffield he wrote that Stevenson became my close and valued friend. He was a lovely man. The fine, sharp, informed, and humorous quality of his mind was unique among public men I have known...He was a great man but he was also our friend...and then suddenly he was dead, and we had that sort of hollow, gray feeling in the pit of the stomach... Strange how selfish one becomes about one's friends. (827)

Steinbeck had lost a friend. Understanding the depth of that loss is difficult to gauge. His admiration for Stevenson was anchored in the civility which Stevenson brought to public life and, importantly, to private relationships as well. After the electoral defeat in 1952, Steinbeck had written to him:

Men of ideals and conscience avoided politics as an arena where wolves tore at the body of the nation and snapped and snarled at each other. Then in a few short months, you...changed that picture. You made it seem possible for politics to be as it once had been, an honorable, virtuous, and creative business. ("The Stevenson Spirit" 334)

The John Steinbeck of the 1950s was not attracted to politics by the principles and ideals as expressed in the ideology of either major American political party. In Warren French's view, Steinbeck left the impression that there was "no fundamental ideological difference" between Democrats and Republicans and that his allegiance was, rather, to men (French 297); more loyalty to men than to party, more loyalty to Adlai Stevenson than to most men in public life. He saw in Stevenson the virtues and ideals of conscience, dignity, and honor; values perhaps planted in an understanding of the American character shared by Stevenson and Steinbeck. In a very real sense, they both believed, as Stevenson said in a 1955 speech, that "Americans have never lived by bread alone. We have lived by ideals and moral values" (Polley 29).

Steinbeck scholar E.W. Tedlock was prophetic when in 1957 he wrote that "Steinbeck's greatest contribution may turn out to be the exploration and colonization of the no man's land between intellectual and non-intellectual" (Tedlock xxix). In the end, the Stevenson-Steinbeck relationship did seem, indeed, to embody the often-difficult reconciliation of two tensions, the creative and the political. In 1965 both John Steinbeck and Archibald MacLeish, the political artists, mourned not just a politician, but an honorable friend, who through the medium of politics had articulately conveyed ennobling attitudes and qualities rarely found in Presidential politics.

Assorted Stevenson campaign buttons from 1952 and 1956

CHAPTER 7

Conclusion

Abstract What can one conclude about the relationship between Adlai Stevenson and American intellectuals? The answer lies in the two emergent themes in this study. On the one hand, evidence yields criticism of both Stevenson and intellectuals, and of the relationship between the two. On the other hand, the same record points to a relationship which reflects credit on both.

Keywords Wit • Comparison • Trusted • Respectability • Alienation • Flirtation • Contradiction

> *Let four captains*
> *Bear Hamlet like a soldier to the stage,*
> *For he was likely, had he been put on,*
> *To have proved most royally....*
> —Fortinbras in *Hamlet*
> Act 5, sc. 2, lines 410–413

What can one conclude about the relationship between Adlai Stevenson and American intellectuals? The answer lies in the two emergent themes in this study. On the one hand, evidence yields criticism of both Stevenson and intellectuals, and of the relationship between the two. On the other

C. B. Bultman, *Adlai E. Stevenson and American Intellectuals*,
https://doi.org/10.1007/978-3-031-80648-3_7

hand, the same record points to a relationship which reflects credit on both.

This investigation affirms that Stevenson, though he garnered the affinity of intellectuals, was himself not an intellectual, as commonly and narrowly defined. That is, Stevenson did not commit his life to focusing on ideas and/or creative works *for their own sake*. Thus defined, he was, in short, neither a scholar nor a creative thinker.

However, when applying the inclusive definition of an intellectual suggested in Chap. 1, namely, someone who sustains the sovereignty of intellect and/or imagination, Stevenson comes closer to warranting description as an intellectual. He did reveal habits of the mind that were contemplative, critical, and on occasion, creative. He also had an enormous curiosity, a devotion to humanism and the struggle for liberty.

Furthermore, if one looks beyond this still quite general means of defining an intellectual to social fact, Stevenson may, finally, qualify. "In social fact...an intellectual is often one who simply identifies himself as an intellectual, participates with other intellectuals in discussions of questions that are deemed intellectual, and is confirmed in that status by those who are recognized, informally, as the leaders of the intellectual world" (Bullock 315). Adlai Stevenson did, on occasion, refer to himself as an intellectual. He certainly participated with intellectuals in discussions of intellectual questions. But the last part of this definition is more critical to my point. Stevenson was "confirmed" in the status of intellectual by more narrowly defined intellectuals themselves. As we have seen, they praised him, promoted him, and in some ways, created him in their own image. Stevenson was, perhaps, the symbol of an intellectual without actually being one.

Another problematic definition in any treatment of Adlai Stevenson is that of "liberal," particularly in the accusatory tone applied by those who thought Stevenson was not "liberal" enough. Though liberalism evolved in earlier centuries to emphasize the individual developing free from government interference, in the twentieth century it has come to mean support for government as a positive force in solving social and economic problems, for government as an agent for equality and social welfare, while at the same time maintaining the traditional concern for personal rights.

Criticism of Stevenson for not falling neatly into modern programmatic liberalism lends itself to a study separate from this one. But an argument could be made that Stevenson was somehow caught between this modern liberalism and a liberalism in what Irving Howe once called its "heroic phase." In its "heroic phase" (the eighteenth and much of the nineteenth centuries), liberalism was not a mere program for social change, or a political movement advancing that program (Howe, *Literature and Liberalism* xii). Rather, it was liberalism as "a new historic temper, a turning of minds to openness of idea and variousness of sentiment...with respect for all living beings, belief in human potential, appreciation for the differences among us that go deep...an awareness of the need for compassionate solidarity in facing the terribleness of life" (xiii).

Stevenson himself may have recognized a changing mood toward the perpetual reforms of contemporary liberalism. In a 1952 speech Stevenson remarked that "The strange alchemy of time has somehow converted the Democrats into the truly conservative party of this country...the party dedicated to conserving all that is best, and building solidly on these foundations" (Hofstadter, *The Paranoid Style in American Politics* 43). One wonders if Stevenson did not have in mind many of the "foundations" formed in the heroic phase of liberalism. One wonders, too, if a liberal critique of Stevenson in the 1950s may ask too much of him and too much of liberalism as well.

Despite these definitional complexities, this study does verify that intellectuals, by and large, supported Stevenson more intensely and with more vigor than they had supported a presidential candidate in many years, even under the suspicion that he was not, by some accounts, an intellectual. To be sure, Franklin Roosevelt had attracted the interest and support of intellectuals during his thirteen-year tenure as President. Roosevelt's professorial brains trust, as well as the creative writers who worked in his behalf, were welcome in the White House. Historian Paul Conkin assessed that they provided him with "delightful conversation" and "were tools for his enjoyment" (Conkin 13). In return, Roosevelt "exalted them into seats of importance" (14).

Many of these same intellectuals, no doubt, later flocked to Stevenson's campaigns. Some who did, as I have pointed out, went beyond merely supporting him for election. They were devoted, devoted not to the excitement of manipulating the strings of national policy, but to Adlai Stevenson.

Although he was clearly not anti-intellectual, Roosevelt never claimed to be an intellectual and was never seen as one. Intellectuals supported him anyway. Stevenson, on the other hand, was frequently perceived as intellectual by anti-intellectuals and intellectuals alike, and perhaps even thought of himself as one. Some intellectuals went so far as to compare him to the premier intellect among presidents, Thomas Jefferson. Brooks

Atkinson of *The New York Times*, for example, wrote that he "never expected in a political campaign to hear America discussed in terms of the dreams of Jefferson" (220). Nicole Tucci of *The New Yorker* commented that "Stevenson is the first great optimist after Jefferson, the first real *grand seigneur* of our age.... Jefferson had come back, we had not lost our friend, here he was in his unchanged antiquity...repairing and sharpening the dusty weapons of the great wise men in history" (208). And Dumas Malone, prolific and sustaining Jefferson biographer, recalled that the Stevenson presidential campaign in 1952 was "one that will always remain with me, along with the conviction that he [Stevenson] emerged from it as the most appealing public figure of my time" (377). Stevenson was elsewhere described as having "the Enlightenment's cool Deist religion, its belief in reason and the possibility of progress, its fundamental optimism and intellectual curiosity" (Ward 216).

Yet, in the last analysis, Stevenson biographers, many of them intellectuals who had supported Stevenson, agreed that he was not truly an intellectual, and certainly not Jefferson reincarnate. Ken Hechler, research assistant to President Truman, wrote that "the most difficult area to assess in Stevenson's legacy is his intellectual brilliance. Very few faculty members at Princeton University...could recall him scholastically as being much more than an indifferent, average, student" (Liebling 52). Was the pervasive admiration for Stevenson among intellectuals, then, based on misunderstanding? Were they attracted to him largely because they really thought he was just like them? Not solely. As I have shown, there were several ingredients which fostered the alignment between intellectuals and Stevenson, not the least of them a genuine, mutual respect. In Chaps. 4 and 5 one sees a mutual respect that was not only genuine, but deeply personal as well.

Was this alignment good for Stevenson? Was it good for the intellectuals who had laid their claim to him? And, was it ultimately good for the country? Ambiguity persists, particularly in any attempt to answer the last of these questions.

Stevenson's connection to intellectuals appeared, at times, to be his life-blood. The numerous occasions on which he either pined for their company or demanded their correspondence reflects a sometimes-desperate attempt to value himself only as much as intellectuals valued him. Courting them, it seems, frequently became an end in itself. Does this mean that Stevenson, as historian, moralist, and social critic, Christopher Lasch said of Theodore Roosevelt's bond with intellectuals at the turn of the century, disowned "the manifestations of the culture of the middle class" (Lasch 254)? I do not think so. Even as he sought out intellectuals, and worked so hard to identify with them, Stevenson maintained, if not an exactly middle-class existence, one that was "middlebrow." In other words, he never totally "threw in" with the elites and was no soldier in a culture war.

This is not to say that Stevenson never willingly presented himself as someone who was at least influenced by intellectuals in "high culture." In fact, he relished occasions on which he expected to be contrasted with other politicians who were perceived as less erudite. Consider as an example one component of the intellectual persona, wit. Stevenson's wit was well received by intellectuals, and he knew it. He reveled in being able to subtly turn a phrase that may have brought smiles and smirks from intellectuals, but left other citizens confused. Wit, which by definition is humor intellectualized, had its drawbacks on Stevenson's campaign trail. In fact, columnist Godrey Sperling, in an election year warning to candidates, referred to the negative perception in this regard, writing that "before long many voters began to think he [Stevenson] was more a funny man than presidential material and that he was trivializing his candidacy" (Sperling 19).

While Stevenson and his intellectual friends bantered and flattered, political insiders often lamented and fretted. In 1956, Stevenson's campaign manager, Jim Finnegan, voiced such frustration. "We had two groups of people supposedly joined in running this campaign," recalled Finnegan,

> There were the politicians and the intellectuals. And for some reason, the politicians were determined to try and make decisions as if they were intellectuals. And the intellectuals insisted on trying to think and act like politicians. What the hell could one expect? (McKeever 379)

Stevenson's invitation to intellectuals to join his political battles certainly exacted a price from both, and the confusion of which Finnegan spoke, and the disorientation it may have caused the campaign effort is a good example.

At the core of these kinds of criticism leveled at Stevenson and intellectuals, and at their relationship, is a severe case of romantic projections suffered by both.

Stevenson believed that the nation shared, or at the very least ought to share, his devotion to civility, devotion which included respect for the role of intellectuals in politics. Intellectuals in politics, thought Stevenson, would create a new political climate, or perhaps return to an old one, which promoted a certain national sophistication. This, of course, was not to be in the 1950s. Many among the general voting public found Stevenson's behavior supercilious beyond acceptance. They saw him as fastidious, as priggish, especially in contrast to the "manly" General Eisenhower. In failing to win the grand prize, Stevenson was a "romantic projection of their [intellectuals'] own powerlessness" (Carter 153), as well as a symbol of much of what the public at large despised about intellectuals.

Likewise, intellectuals believed that their association with Stevenson would carve out a spot for them on the national stage. Campaign for Stevenson, write for Stevenson, correspond with Stevenson, be seen with Stevenson, and the result, they suspected, would be a Stevenson White House that was also their White House.

Later, as the John F. Kennedy presidency unfolded, many intellectuals anticipated the sense of power they never fully realized with Stevenson. But, as Christopher Lasch pointed out, the relationship, in many respects, served to further destroy the intellectual because the intellectual life "had become bound up with images of worldly success and prestige" (Lasch 313). The intellectuals' alignment with Kennedy produced "a cultural tone of Broadway sophistication" (321) that was more glitz and glamour than it was thoughtful and reflective. Lasch describes as "disheartening" the "desperate gratitude with which intellectuals welcomed even a few crumbs from the presidential table" (311), willingly prostituted just because someone had asked.

Whether or not a Stevenson presidency, replete with intellectuals as advisors and as companions, would have mirrored the Kennedy experience is uncertain. Critics of Stevenson and his alliance with intellectuals would argue that moving the relationship to center stage could have been even more destructive. If intellectuals in the brief Kennedy years lost intellectuality because they were "glamorized" by the bright lights of national attention, Kennedy himself was not rendered politically ineffective by that development. Given Stevenson's penchant for *le haute monde*, intellectuals who frequented a Stevenson White House would have run the risk of being "glamorized" at the expense of substantive contributions to public policy; this, in addition to the more general charge of selling creative genius for inclusion in the affairs of state.

Furthermore, because Stevenson was prone to lonely brooding, to a sort of restless despair, his relations with others, especially intellectuals, were inherently more important to him than they were to Kennedy. Whereas Kennedy was able to move from the political tensions of the Oval Office to the salon events of the East Room with relative ease, Stevenson appeared so emotionally linked to intellectuals like MacLeish and Steinbeck that one rightly wonders if Stevenson was truly capable of gaining from their creative input, while admitting that there might be limitations in their political contributions.

Similarly, one could accurately assume that Stevenson's close friendships with intellectuals would have, at times, favored private musings and public literary allusion making over clear-headed political judgments. After all, Stevenson was often preoccupied with frequent, and often sustained communication with intellectuals; communication that was not always about the intricacies of public policy, as documented throughout this book. Such intense emotional and psychological dependency, then, could be taken as a likely distraction to governing effectively.

Yet, this same intense emotional and psychological dependency offered something positive for Stevenson, the intellectuals, and the country. Intellectuals in in Stevenson's day were eager to escape "from the isolation to which intellectuality seemed to condemn them" (64). Politics was "how people sorted themselves, what they talked about, how they judged the world" (Laskin 79). To be nothing more than a casual observer to the great events of the post-war period was simply not enough for many intellectuals, Archibald MacLeish, and John Steinbeck among them.

American poet and essayist, Adrienne Rich, in writing about poetry and politics over the last few decades, discussed the need for political involvement by creative writers such as herself in a recent book. Four decades ago, Rich wrote that a poet "must be twice-born. She must have begun as a poet, she must have understood the suffering of the world as political, and have gone through politics, and on the other side of politics she must be reborn again as a poet" (Rich 21). In 1993, Rich revisited her earlier statement and revised it, now believing that the goal is "finding the relationship" between poetry and politics (21). In her first assessment, Rich concluded that politics was something to "have gone through," something to arrive on "the other side" of, and in doing so become a better poet. Her revision is particularly interesting to me because it implies a permanence and power to the "convergence of the engaged political life with the unwavering conscience, and the impassioned imagination" (St. Jean 223).

Stevenson played a significant role in making more permanent and powerful "the engaged political life" of many intellectuals. He drew creative and academic intellectuals into politics and into public notice, and though MacLeish and Steinbeck, for example, were disdained by numerous peers, on the most personal level, the process ushered in for them a reign of respectability. That respectability had little to do with the accumulation of political power through their association with Adlai Stevenson; in the end there was not much to accumulate.

Central to this respectability, I believe, was the critical admission by intellectuals supporting Stevenson that a life worth living is honed by a balance between the heart and the head. For many of them, Stevenson was the catalyst for just such an admission. After Stevenson died, Eric Sevareid wrote that Stevenson had made him "feel importantly alive" and "trusted." Sevareid continued the acknowledgment with the following words.

> I am cursed with a somewhat forbidding Scandinavian manner, with a restraint that spells stuffiness to a lot of people. But Adlai saw through all that unfortunate façade. He knew that inside I am mush, full of a lot of almost pathetic sentimentality about this country, the Midwest, Abraham Lincoln, and the English language...He was what the French call "a friend of the heart" because he saw through to your heart. (Johnson 8: 844)

Exposing the heart is often difficult for intellectuals. Many retire to ivory towers where they can claim critical purity and find solace in alienation.

I do not believe that the intellectuals who supported Stevenson's candidacies "sold out" to, nor "caved in" to politics. Nor do I believe that Stevenson avoided the "real" world of politics in lieu of an often isolated, melancholic, alienated world of books. His flirtation with intellectuals did not make him a Henry James character in a Joseph Heller world, as one writer described him (Morgan 53). Neither did his bond with intellectuals exalt him to the status of a prince among plain men, any more than it exposed him to be, in the words of Secretary of State Dean Rusk, "a plain man among princes" (Graff 35). Stevenson's friend Agnes Meyer was correct when she referred to him as a bowl of contradictions. He was, for example, sensitive in his compassion for citizens in the underdeveloped world, but sophisticated in his ability to float easily in the most formal of settings. He was liberal in his devotion to the United Nations and his repudiation of McCarthyism, just as he was politically conservative on certain civil rights issues, and hardly progressive in some social views. He was philosophical in his reflection on moral questions, while practical in the mundane work of political precincts and union halls. And, he was intellectual in his passion for learning and admiration for intellectuals themselves, but anti-intellectual in the absence of personal scholarship and creative genius. In the end, intellectuals like MacLeish and Steinbeck accepted the ambiguities in Stevenson because they resembled their own.

John Kenneth Galbraith highlighted the complexity and ambiguity in the relationships between Stevenson and intellectuals in his memoirs. Recalling Stevenson's campaigns, he wrote: "People who were close to F.D.R. or J.F.K. found much pleasure in explaining their President to outsiders. Those of us around Stevenson spent much of our time explaining him to each other" (Galbraith, *A Life In Our Times* 287). Addressing the Law and Legal Clubs of Chicago less than a year after Adlai Stevenson's death, Judge Carl McGowen, the well-known politico, and Stevenson friend said, "It [the lure of Stevenson] exists as one of the most extraordinary phenomena of the political life of our time. Reams remain to be written about it by future historians and political scientists. It is undoubtably too early to articulate the final and definitive explanation of why it was so" (Liebling 201).

Stevenson's friend Barbara Ward once described his greatest gift as "nommo," which is the Bantu word for the quality of "making life rather larger and more vivid for everyone else" (Ward 212). Is that not one of the good things that literature can accomplish as well, even the literature of Archibald MacLeish and John Steinbeck? I believe it is. I also believe that Adlai Stevenson's "nommo" left an impression of goodness that in many ways pleasantly surprised intellectuals. His kind of wisdom rested in "a clear intelligence, informed by a sufficient awareness of complexity and difficulty, sobered by a tragic sense, *but* [emphasis mine] sweetened by a spirit of faith, hope, and charity" (Muller 326). This was a wisdom many intellectuals could accept because it was their type of wisdom too.

That Adlai Stevenson so profoundly affected American intellectuals posed a problem for them. Eric Sevareid put it this way: "So, like a good many other people, I will never forget this man. But I will never fall in love with a politician again. I haven't the right to, in my kind of work, and there is too much pain in it" (Johnson 8: 845). Whether or not Stevenson would "have proved most royally" is open to question, but when Archibald

MacLeish, John Steinbeck, and others bore him "to the stage," the pain they felt was tempered by the knowledge that they had been part of a very important relationship. Alfred Kazan again: "The extraordinary identification that so many American intellectuals make with Stevenson has often struck me as loyalty not to a lost cause but to lostness as a cause...cherished more for his sensitivity than for the strength of his ideas" (Solotaroff 134).

The relationships between MacLeish and Stevenson, and Steinbeck and Stevenson, were personal only because they were public. For MacLeish, Stevenson enriched his time because he gave himself "in thought and action, not to his friends alone, but to the country, to his world" (Johnson 8: vii). For Steinbeck, Stevenson became "the representation...of American politics brought to its highest honor" (Benson 971) by transforming the political arena from a place "where wolves tore at the body of the nation" to a "virtuous and creative business" ("The Stevenson Spirit" 334). These are strong sentiments, indeed. They were, in fact, the "terms of endearment." Despite legitimate criticism of the political and personal Adlai Stevenson, he elevated among intellectuals the will to become contemporary, to become intensely involved in our world through politics. He also heightened among them the attitude that doing so is not merely a privilege, but a responsibility. That elevation of will and commitment, I believe, was good for Stevenson, good for intellectuals, and inasmuch as a democracy truly flowers only with full participation of all its people, including intellectuals, the elevation was also good for the country.

WORKS CITED

Aaron, Daniel. *Writers On The Left*. New York: Harcourt, Brace and World, Inc. 1961.

Adell, Nicholas. "The Shadow of Adlai Stevenson," in historynetworknews.org/article/the-shadow-of-adlai-stevenson, 2024.

Adlai Stevenson Project, "Marietta Tree," Oral History Research Office, Columbia University, 1968, 92–93.

Adler, Bill, *The Stevenson Wit*. Garden City, New York: Doubleday and Company, Inc., 1966.

Aldrich, John W. "Foreword" in *The Politics of Twentieth Century Novelists*, ed. by George Panichas. New York: Thomas Y. Crowell Company, 1974, pp. vii–xxii.

Anderson, Patrick. *The President's Men*. Garden City, N.Y: Doubleday, 1968.

Apple, R.W., Jr., "Elected Bodies With Hardly a Cultured Bone." *The New York Times*, July 26, 1998, sec. 2, p. 2

Attwood, William. "Pencils, Pads and Chronic Stamina," in *As We Knew Adlai: The Stevenson Story by Twenty-Two Friends*, ed. by Edward P. Doyle, New York: Harper and Row, 1966.

Arvey, Jacob. "A Gold Nugget in Your Backyard," in *As We Knew Adlai: The Stevenson Story by Twenty-Two Friends*, ed. by Edward P. Doyle. New York: Harper and Row, 1966.

Bailey, Thomas. *Presidential Greatness*. New York: Appleton-Century Press, 1966.

Baker, Carlos, ed. *Ernest Hemingway: Selected Letters 1917-1961*. New York: Charles Scribner's Sons, 1981.

Baker, Jean H. *The Stevensons: A Biography of An American Family*. New York: W.W. Norton & Company, 1996.

© The Author(s), under exclusive license to Springer Nature Switzerland AG 2025
C. B. Bultman, *Adlai E. Stevenson and American Intellectuals*,
https://doi.org/10.1007/978-3-031-80648-3

Ball, George. "With AES in War and Politics," in *As We Knew Adlai: The Stevenson Story by Twenty-Two Friends,* ed. by Edward P. Doyle. New York: Harper and Row, 1966.

Barber, James David. *The Presidential Character.* Englewood Cliffs: Prentice Hall, 1972.

Bakewell, Sarah. *At The Existentialist Café: Freedom, Being, and Apricot Cocktails.* New York: Other Press, 2016.

Bensen, Jackson J. *The True Adventures of John Steinbeck, Writer.* New York: The Viking Press, 1984.

Berman, Ronald. *America in The Sixties: An Intellectual History.* New York: Harper and Row, 1968.

Bien, Peter. "Nikos Kazantzakis," in *The Politics of Twentieth Century Novelists* ed. by George Panichas. New York: Thomas Y. Crowell Company, 1974, pp. 137–159.

Blum, John Morton. *V Was for Victory.* Boston: Houghton Mifflin Company, 1974.

Brademas, John. "Stevenson: His Impact on Education, International Affairs, Nixon, and American Politics," in *Adlai Stevenson's Lasting Legacy,* ed. by Alvin Liebling. New York: Palgrave Macmillan, 2007.

Branch, Taylor. *Parting The Waters: America in The King years 1954-1963.* New York: Simon and Shuster, 1988.

Brightman, Carol, ed. *Between Friends: The Correspondence of Hannah Arendt and Mary McCarthy.* New York: Harcourt, Brace & Company, 1995.

Brock, William. "Americanism," in *The United States A Companion To American Studies,* ed. by Dennis Willand. London: Methuen Publishers, 1974.

Brodie, Fawn. *Richard Nixon: The Shaping of His Character.* New York: W.W. Norton and Company, 1981.

Brogan, Denis. "The Intellectual in Great Britain," in *The Intellectual in Politics,* ed. by H. Malcolm MacDonald. Austin: The University of Texas Press, 1966, pp. 60–73.

Brooks, Van Wyck. "Highbrow and Lowbrow," in *America's Coming of Age.* New York: B.W. Huebsch, 1915.

Brooks, Van Wyck. "Where Are Our Intellectuals?" in *The Freeman II,* September 29, 1920, pp. 53–54.

Brown, Michael J. *Hope and Scorn: Eggheads, Experts, and Elites in American Politics.* Chicago: University of Chicago Press, 2020.

Bruccoli, Matthew, and Margaret M. Duggan. *Correspondence of F. Scott Fitzgerald.* New York: Random House, 1980.

Brustein, Robert. "The Curse of Official Cultures," in *Literature and Liberalism* ed. by Edward Zwick. Washington, D.C: The New Republic Book Company, Inc., 1976, pp. 159–164.

Bullock, Alan and Oliver Stallybrass, eds. *The Harper Dictionary of Modern Thought.* New York: Harper and Row, Publishers, 1977.

Campbell, Angus. *The American Voter*. New York: John Wiley and Sons, Inc., 1964.

Carr, Virginia Spencer. *The Lonely Hunter: A Biography of Carson McCullers*. New York: Doubleday, 1975.

Carter, Paul. *Another Part of The Fifties*. New York: Columbia University, 1983.

Cattini, Richard. "The Poet As Centurion," *The Christian Science Monitor*, May 12, 1992.

Coles, Robert. *The Political Life of Children*. Boston: Houghton, Mifflin, and Company, 1986.

Conkin, Paul K. *The New Deal*. New York: Thomas Y. Crowell Company, Inc., 1967.

Cooke, Alistair. "Adlai Stevenson: The Failed Saint," in *Six Great Men*. New York: Random House, 1977.

Corporation for Public Broadcasting. *Adlai E. Stevenson: The Man from Libertyville*. [Documentary Film] 1990.

Cowley, Malcolm. *And I Worked At The Writer's Trade: Chapters in Literary History, 1919-1978*. New York: The Viking Press, 1978.

Cowley, Malcolm. "Exile's Return," in *Literature and Liberalism* ed. by Edward Zwick. Washington, D.C: The New Republic Book Club, Inc., 1976a, pp. 218–222.

Cowley, Malcolm. "To A Revolutionary Critic," in *Literature and Liberalism*, ed. by Edward Zwick. Washington D.C: The New Republic Book Club, Inc., 1976b, pp. 202–204.

Curtis, Cathy. *A Splendid Intelligence: The Life of Elizabeth Hardwick*. New York: W.W. Norton and Company, 2022.

Davis, Kenneth S. *The Politics of Honor*. New York: Putnam, 1967.

DeMott, Benjamin. "Archibald MacLeish," in *Poets At Work The Paris Review Interviews*, ed. by George Plimpton. New York: Penguin Books, 1989.

Dick, Jane Warner. "Forty Years of Friendship," in *As We Knew Adlai: The Stevenson Story by Twenty-Two Friends*, ed. by Edward p. Doyle. New York: Harper and Row, 1966.

Doherty, Maggie. "Duty Dancing: How Seamus Heaney Wrote His Way Through A War." Book Review in *The New Yorker*, September 9, 2024. p. 63.

Donaldson, Scott. *Archibald MacLeish : An American Life*. Boston: Houghton Mifflin Company, 1992.

Donnelly, Honoria Murphy. *Sara and Gerald*. New York: Holt, Rinehart and Winston, 1984.

Douglas, George H. *Edmund Wilson's America*. Lexington, Kentucky: The University of Kentucky Press, 1983.

"Eggheads: Cracking the Enigma." *Newsweek*, October 8, 1956, pp. 53–57.

Farber, Bernard, ed. *Adlai Stevenson*. Leiber-Stoller Production, Red Bird Recording, 20–105, 1965.

Fairlie, Henry. Review of *Adlai Stevenson: His Life and Legacy*, by Porter McKeever. *The New Republic*, July 17 & 24, 1989, pp. 27–30.

Fentress, Calvin. "At the 1952 Democratic Convention, I Witnessed Honest Politics," in digitaledition.chicagotribune.com/infinity/article, August 21, 2024.

Fitch, Robert E. "Intellectual in Defeat." *Christian Century*, November 26, 1952, pp. 1377–1379.

French, Warren. "John Steinbeck," in *The Politics of Twentieth Century Novelists*, ed. by George Panichas. New York: Thomas Y. Crowell Company, 1974.

Galbraith, John Kenneth. *The Age of Uncertainty*. Boston: Houghton Mifflin Company, 1977.

Galbraith, John Kenneth. *A Life In Our Times*. Boston: Houghton Mifflin Company, 1981.

Gass, William H. "The Artist and Society," *The New Republic*, July 27, 1968, p. 16.

Gilbert, James. *Another Chance: Post-war America 1945-1968*. New York: Alfred A. Knopf, Inc. 1981.

Ginzburg, Benjamin. *The New Republic*, February 18, 1931, pp. 15–17.

Gold, Arthur. "They Liked Adlai." *Washingtonian*, October 1992, p. 23.

Goldman, Eric F. *The Crucial Decade and After: America 1945-1960*. New York: Vintage Books, 1960.

Goodwin, Doris Kearns. *An Unfinished Love Affair: A Personal History of the Sixties*. New York: Simon & Shuster, 2024.

Goodwin, Richard. *Remembering America*. Boston: Little, Brown and Company, 1988.

Graff, Leo. "Why They Were Madly for Adlai." *The Grand Rapids Press*, November 18, 1979, pp. 34–35.

Halberstam, David. *The Best and The Brightest*. New York: Random House, 1972.

Hamilton, Ian. *Robert Lowell*. New York: Random House, 1982.

Havel, Vaclav. "A Farewell to Politics." *New York Review of Books* October 24, 2002.

Hechler, Ken. "Stevenson: Concerned and Brilliant, His Finest Hour Was In Seeking a Nuclear Test Ban," in *Adlai Stevenson's Lasting Legacy*, ed. by Alvin Liebling. New York: Palgrave Macmillan, 2007.

Hofstadter, Richard. *Anti-Intellectualism in American Life*. New York: Alfred A. Knopf, Inc., 1963.

Hofstadter, Richard. *The Paranoid Style in American Politics*. New York: Vintage Books, 1967.

Howe, Irving. Introduction. *Literature and Liberalism*, ed. by Edward Zwick. Washington, D.C: The New Republic Book Club, Inc., 1976, p. xiii.

Howe, Irving. *Steady Work*. New York: Harcourt, Brace, and World, Inc., 1966.

Howe, Irving. "Stevenson and the Intellectuals." *Dissent*, Winter: Issue 1, 1954. Reprinted August 1, 2008.

Ives, Elizabeth Stevenson, and Hildegard Dolson. *My Brother Adlai*. New York: William Morrow, 1956.

Jackson, Joseph Henry. Introduction. *The Short Novels of John Steinbeck*. New York: The Viking Press, 1953.

Jay, Paul, ed. *The Selected Letters of Kenneth Burke and Malcolm Cowley 1915-1981*. New York: Viking Press, 1988.

Johnson, Walter, ed. *The Papers of Adlai E. Stevenson. 8 vols*. Boston: Little, Brown, and Company, 1977.

Karl, Frederick R. *William Faulkner: American Writer*. New York: Ballantine Books, 1989.

Key, V.O. *Politics, Parties and Pressure Groups*. New York: Thomas Y. Crowell, 1964.

Kiernan, Thomas. *The Intricate Muse: A Biography of John Steinbeck*. Boston: Little, Brown and Company, 1979.

Kidder, Rushworth M. "Eloquence From A Playwright Drenched in Politics." *The Christian Science Monitor*, March 5, 1990, p. 19.

Klinkner, Phillip. "Until 1968," in *The Conversation*, July 21, 2024.

Lamb, Brian, prod. Interview with John Seigenthaler. *Book-notes*, C-SPAN, Washington, D.C., July 22, 1992.

Larsen, Arthur. *The President Nobody Knew*. New York: Charles Scribner's Sons, 1968.

Lasch, Christopher. *The New Radicalism in America 1889-1963*. New York: Alfred A. Knopf, 1965.

Laskin, David. *Partisans: Marriage, Politics, and Betrayal Among the New York Intellectuals*. New York: Simon and Schuster, 2000.

Lee, Hermione. "Tracking The Untouchables." *The New York Review of Books*, pp. 53–57.

Lewis, Clifford. "Political Testaments: John Steinbeck The Artist as FDR Speechwriter," in *Rediscovering Steinbeck Revisionist Views of His Art, Politics and Intellect*, ed. by Clifford Lewis and Carroll Birtch. Lewiston, New York: The Edwin Mellon Press, 1989.

Life Magazine, February 9, 1959, p. 31.

Liebling, Alvin, ed. *Adlai Stevenson's Lasting Legacy*. New York: Palgrave Macmillan, 2007.

Macdonald, Dwight. *Against the American Grain*. New York: Vintage Books, 1965.

Macdonald, Dwight. "Kulturbolsheivismus and Mr. Van Wyk Brooks," in *Memories of a Revolutionist*. New York: Farrar, Strauss and Company, 1957.

MacDonald, H. Malcolm, ed. *The Intellectual in Politics*. Austin: The University of Texas Press, 1966.

MacLeish, Archibald. *A Continuing Journey*. Boston: Houghton Mifflin Co, 1967.

Manchester, William. *The Glory and The Dream A Narrative History of America 1932-1972*. Boston: Little, Brown and Company, 1973.

Marien, Mary Werner. "American Poet of Social Purpose." *The Christian Science Monitor,* May 15, 1992.

Marovitz, Sanford E. "John Steinbeck and Adlai Stevenson: The Shattered Image of America," in *Steinbeck's Literary Dimension: A Guide To Comparative Studies,* ed. by Tetsamuro Hayashi. Metuchen, New Jersey: The Scarecrow Press, Inc., 1973.

Martin, John Bartlow. *Adlai Stevenson of Illinois.* Garden City, New York; Doubleday, 1976.

Martin, John Bartlow. *Adlai Stevenson and The World.* Garden City, New York: Doubleday, 1977.

Martine, James J. "Away From the Writing Table: Politics, Sex, and Other Vices in the Lives of American Writers," in *American Literary Almanac,* ed. by Karen L. Rood. New York: Bruccoli, Clark Layman, Inc., 1988.

Mazzaro, Jerome. *Profile of Robert Lowell.* Columbus, Ohio: Charles E. Merrill Publishing Company, 1971.

McCarthy, Eugene J. *The Hard Years.* New York: Vintage Books, 1975.

McGowen, Carl. "Adlai's Integrity and Credibility Were Impressive National Resources," in *Adlai Stevenson's Lasting Legacy,* ed by Alvin Liebling. New York: Palgrave Macmillan, 2007.

McGrory, Mary. "The Perfectionist and The Press," in *As We Knew Adlai: The Stevenson Story by Twenty-Two Friends,* ed. by Edward P. Doyle. New York: Harper and Row, 1966.

McKeever, Porter. *Adlai Stevenson: His Life and Legacy.* New York: William Morrow and Company, Inc., 1989.

Mehnert, Klaus. "The Weather Makers," in *The Intellectual in Politics,* ed. by H. Malcolm MacDonald. Austin: University of Texas Press, 1966, pp. 90–102.

Mencken, H.L. "On Being An American," in *Prejudices.* New York: Vintage Books, 1958, pp. 49–64.

Morgan, Thomas. "Madly for Adlai," in *American Heritage,* August–September, 1984, pp. 49–64.

Millichap, Joseph R. *Steinbeck and Film.* New York: Frederick Unger Publishing Company, 1982.

Mitgang, Herbert. *Dangerous Dossiers.* New York: Donald I. Fine, Inc., 1988a.

Mitgang, Herbert, ed. *The Letters of Robert Frost.* New York: Harcourt Brace Jovanovich, Publishers, 1988.

Muller, Herbert. *Adlai Stevenson: A Study in Values.* New York: Harper and Row, 1967.

Murse, Tom. "Adlai Ewing Stevenson: An Urbane, Witty, Articulate Politician and Diplomat" in https://www.thoughtco.com/adlai-stevenson-biography-4172626, October 12, 2018.

Natwar-Singh, K. "He Dignified Our Political Dialogue," in *The Saturday Review,* January 1, 1966.

Page, Tim. *Dawn Powell: A Biography.* New York: Henty Holt and Company, 1998.

Panichas, George, ed. *The Politics of Twentieth Century Novelists.* New York: Thomas Y. Crowell Company, 1974.

"Parallels With A Prison." *Newsweek,* July 22, 1991, p. 31.

Pells, Robert H. *The Liberal Mind In A Conservative Age: American Intellectuals in the 1940s and 1950s.* New York: Harper and Row, 1985.

Phillips, Robert, ed. *Letters of Delmore Schwartz.* Princeton: Ontario Review Press, 1977.

Polley, Robert, ed. *Man of Honor, Man of Peace: The Life and Words of Adlai Stevenson.* New York: G.P. Putnam's Sons, 1965.

Rabinowitch, Eugene. Eulogy for Adlai Stevenson in *The Bulletin of American Scientists,* September, 1965.

Rich, Adrienne. *What Is Found There: Notebooks on Poetry and Politics.* New York: W.W. Norton and Company, 1993.

Roberts, David. *Jean Stafford: A Biography.* London: Chatts and Windus, 1988.

Ross, Lillian. *Adlai Stevenson.* Philadelphia: J.B. Lippincott Company, 1966.

St. Jean, David. Review of *What I Found There: Notebooks on Poetry and Politics,* by Adrieene Rich. Book Jacket, 1993.

Sandburg, Carl. Text of speech on 25 October 1952. Normal, Illinois. Adlai Stevenson Papers. Illinois State University.

Saroyan, William. LIBQuotes.com/WilliamSaroyan/quoteLB171.

Saturday Review, 13 May 1961.

Schlesinger, Arthur M., Jr. "Politics and Social Change: 1941-1968," in *Interpreting American History: Conversations With Historians Part II,* ed. by John Garraty. New York: Macmillan Company, 1970, pp. 265–288.

Schlesinger, Arthur M., Jr. *Robert Kennedy and His Times. Vol. II.* Boston: Houghton, Mifflin Company, 1978.

Schwarz, Nancy Lynn. *The Hollywood Writers' Wars.* New York: Alfred A. Knopf, Inc., 1982.

Sevareid, Eric. "The Final Troubled Hours of Adlai Stevenson." *Look,* November 30, 1965, pp. 80–86.

Severn, Bill. *Adlai Stevenson: Citizen of The World.* New York: David McKay Company, Inc., 1966.

Shakespeare, William. *The Tragedy of Hamlet,* in *The Yale Shakespeare,* ed. by Wilber L. Cross and Tucker Brooke. New York: Barnes and Noble Books, 1993 p.1082.

Sherwood, Robert. Letter to Adlai Stevenson, 26 July 1952. Normal, Illinois. Adlai Stevenson Papers. Illinois State University.

Sievers, Rodney M. *The Last Puritan? Adlai Stevenson in American Politics.* Port Washington, N.Y.: Associated Faculty Press, Inc., 1983.

Simon, Paul. "Young People Loved Him," in *As We Knew Adlai: The Stevenson Story by Twenty-Two Friends*, ed. by Edward P. Doyle. New York: Harper and Row, 1966.

Smith, Richard Norton. "Silver Tongues and Sharp Elbows." *The Christian Science Monitor*, January 30, 2000, sec. 4, p. 15.

Solotaroff, Ted, ed. *Alfred Kazin's America: Critical and Personal Writings*. New York: Haper Collins, 2003.

Sperling, Godfrey. "Bob Dole's Biting Humor." *The Christian Science Monitor*, October 18, 1994, p. 19.

Sperling, Godfrey. "A Newsman's Take on Newsmakers." *The Christian Science Monitor*, February 4, 1997, p. 19.

Steele, John. *Life*, July 23, 1965, p. 3.

Steinbeck, Elaine and Wallston, Robert, eds. *Steinbeck: A Life in Letters*. New York: The Viking Press, 1975.

Steinbeck, John. Foreword. *Speeches of Adlai Stevenson*. New York: Random House, 1952.

Steinbeck, John. Letter to William Blair, 22 June 1958 (marked confidential). Normal, Illinois. Adlai Stevenson Papers. Illinois State University.

Steinbeck, John. *The Short Reign of Pippin IV A Fabrication*. The Viking Press, 1957.

Steinbeck, John. *The Winter of Our Discontent*. New York: The Viking Press, 1961.

Steinbeck, John. "The Stevenson Spirit," in *The Faces of Five Decades, Selected From Fifty Years of the New Republic 1944-1953*, ed. by Robert B. Luce. New York: Simon Shuster, 1953, pp. 333–334.

Stevenson, Adlai. *Friends and Enemies What I Learned in Russia*. New York: Harper and Brothers, Publishers, 1958.

Stevenson, Adlai. *Looking Outward*, ed. by Robert L. and Selma Schiffer. New York: Harper and Row, 1963.

Stevenson, Adlai. "Robert Frost At Eighty-Eight," in *The New Republic*, 9 April 1962, p. 27.

Stone, I.F. *The Haunted Fifties*. Boston: Little, Brown and Company, 1963.

Sullivan, Louis. *Kindergarten Chats and Other Writings*. New York: Dover Publications, Inc., 1979.

Tedlock, E.W., and C.V. Walker. *Steinbeck and His Critics*. Albuquerque: University of New Mexico, 1957.

Tinder, Glenn. "Can We Be Good Without God," in *The Atlantic*, December, 1989, pp. 69–85.

Trilling, Lionel. "Reality in America," in *The Liberal Imagination*. New York: The Viking Press, 1950, pp. 14–32.

Truman, Margaret, ed. *Where The Buck Stops: The Personal and Private Writings Of Harry S. Truman*. New York: Warner Books, Inc, 1989.

Tullis, Jeffrey. *The Rhetorical Presidency.* Princeton: Princeton University Press, 1987.

Wagner-Martin, Linda. *Sylvia Plath: A Biography.* New York: Simon and Shuster, 1987.

Walton, Richard. *Remnants of Power.* New York: Coward, McGann Inc., 1968.

Ward, Barbara. "Affection and Always Respect," in *As We Knew Adlai: The Stevenson Story by Twenty-Two Friends,* ed. by Edward P. Doyle. New York: Harper and Row, 1966.

Weinstein, Allen. *Perjury: The Hiss-Chambers Case.* New York: Alfred A. Knopf, 1978.

Weiss, Andrea. *Paris Was a Women: Portraits From The Left Bank.* San Francisco: Harper Collins Publishers, 1995.

White, Theodore. *America in Search of Itself: The Making of The President 1956-1980.* New York: Harper and Row, 1982.

"Whose Adlai?" *Time,* October 13, 1952, pp. 29–33.

Will, George. "Al Gore's Liberalism Rooted in Contempt for the Majority." *The Muskegon Chronicle,* June 7, 2000, p. 2A.

Wilson, Edmund. *The Fifties.* New York: Farrar, Strauss, and Giroux, 1986.

Wilson, Edmund. *Classics and Commercials.* New York: Vintage Books, 1962.

Wilson, Elena, ed. *Edmund Wilson: Letters on Literature and Politics 1912-1972.* New York: Farrar, Straus, and Giroux, 1977.

Winnick, Ralph. *Letters of Archibald MacLeish 1907-1982.* Boston: Houghton, Mifflin Company, 1983.

Woodward, C. Vann. *Future of The Past.* New York: Oxford University Press, 1989.

Yates, Norris W. "Gunter Grass," in *The Politics of Twentieth Century Novelists,* ed. by George Panichas. New York: Thomas Y. Crowell Company, 1974, pp. 215–230.

Zizek, Slavoj. Rev. of *Vaclav Havel: A Political Tragedy in Six Acts,* by John Keane. *The London Review of Books* October 28, 1999: 34–36.

INDEX

© The Author(s), under exclusive license to Springer Nature
Switzerland AG 2025
C. B. Bultman, *Adlai E. Stevenson and American Intellectuals*,
https://doi.org/10.1007/978-3-031-80648-3

The manufacturer's authorised representative in the EU is Springer
Nature Customer Service Centre GmbH, Europaplatz 3, 69115 Heidelberg,
Germany. If you have any concerns regarding our products, please
contact ProductSafety@springernature.com

Printed and bound by CPI Group (UK) Ltd, Croydon, CR0 4YY

24/04/2026

02096315-0010